Wonder with the Word

A wayward look at life and the Bible

Dermot Connolly

First published in 2012 by
St. Patrick's Missionary Society,
Kiltegan,
Co. Wicklow
www.spms.org

ISBN 978-0-9574738-0-5

Cover:
The Tree of Life, Batik from The Gambia

Design and layout by Loretta Brennan
Unless otherwise stated, batiks and drawings photographed by Gary Howley SPS,
Martin Smith SPS, Loretta Brennan

Printed in the Republic of Ireland by
Business Print Limited
Unit 3B, Ballymount Industrial Estate
Walkinstown, Dublin 12

For other copyright permissions see page 181.

For
Terry and Padraig
with love

Contents

3: Lent/Easter

The Green Blade Riseth

4: People

Voices in Another Room

5: Liturgy & Seasons

The Gate of Heaven

6: Our World

The Work of Your Hands

7: Stories

As It Happened

A word of welcome and explanation

Concepts create idols; only wonder understands.
Gregory of Nyssa (330–395)

This book began life as a series of articles which appeared between 2001 and 2012 in *Africa*, a monthly magazine produced by St Patrick's Missionary Society. I had done Scripture studies in Rome, and had taught for some years in our seminary in Ireland, but by the time I began this series I had already been living in Nigeria more than twenty-four years. I did not have much access to libraries or books, but I learned from the lives of amazing people all around me. I think that is why these articles are the way they are: wondering with the Word as It weaves through the lives of people, through the Scriptures, through our hearts.

I had no intention of providing a "course of studies" in the Scriptures; the magazine articles were random reflections on various events and experiences, including the Church's liturgy as it unfolded its story throughout the year. For this book I have grouped them under seven themes, but the date of its first publication in *Africa* is appended to each article.

I did have a purpose: to intrigue the readers into going back to the Bible themselves. That is where the living connection is made: not so much in anything I might write, but in the Word of God mediated through the Scriptures. You need to wonder with the Word yourself.

Perhaps I should comment on the way I have written these reflections. I tried to adopt different styles of writing according as a topic, or a passage of Scripture, or even an illustration seemed to demand. I fear it has given a somewhat wayward quality to the collection, but then, that is equally true of both the Jewish and the Christian writings: they contain poetry, drama, narrative, law, lectures, letters, liturgies, stories, visions, songs, curses, arguments.... The Word of God in the Bible comes clothed in the many colours of literature, and has its own sense of style.

The illustrations were always an essential part of the magazine series, and now of the book; without them I would not wish to publish it at all. Pictures may speak where words fail; a number of the batiks here have inspired what I wrote. Besides, some of them are very beautiful. Most were bought in various markets and studios in Nigeria and Cameroon; a few were gifted to me from even farther afield. These are good things out of Africa.

I have people to thank. The editors of *Africa*: Gary Howley (who first inveigled me into writing this series), John P. Carroll, Martin Smith, Tom Kiggins, Loretta Brennan, Tim Redmond. They have all been, as needed, patient, kind, wise and justly critical – good people to work with, on *Africa* magazine, and now on this book. In particular, Loretta's judgement and magical skills with the design and layout have been a wonder to watch.

I have always been graciously uplifted by my own family and friends, and the family of St Patrick's; more than I can mention they have encouraged and guided me. I especially wish to thank Vincent MacNamara who over several years has urged me to put this book together. There were times when he had more faith in it than I had; I am glad his wisdom prevailed.

Dermot Connolly
November 2012

Generally the preferred English translation for Psalms is the Grail (inclusive language version), and for other Scripture quotations, the New Revised Standard Version (NRSV).

Sing Out, My Soul

Sing out, my soul,
sing of the holiness of God:
who has delighted in a woman,
lifted up the poor,
satisfied the hungry,
given voice to the silent,
grounded the oppressor,
blessed the full-bellied with emptiness,
and with the gift of tears
those who have never wept;
who has desired the darkness of the womb,
and inhabited our flesh.
Sing of the longing of God,
sing out, my soul.

Janet Morley

Sing Out, My Soul from *All Desires Known*, Janet Morley

1: Advent/Christmas

A Child is Born

The stories of the birth of Jesus are to be found in the first two chapters of the Gospels of Luke and Matthew; each tells the story in his own way, and sometimes yet other insights can be prompted by a picture or a poem or, for me, a Nigerian batik.

A Batik for Bethlehem

On entering the house, they saw the child with Mary, his mother; and they knelt down and paid him homage. Then, opening their treasure chests, they offered him gifts of gold, frankincense, and myrrh. And having been warned in a dream not to return to Herod, they left for their own country by another road.
(Matthew 2:1-18)

When first I saw this batik of three village women from Nigeria, I thought of Bethlehem. It seemed to me the three women had not come to visit until after the foreigners had gone: wise men, taking the long way home, but with strange ideas of suitable gifts for a young mother and her newborn child. The women, wise in their own ways, brought oil, a fish, and wood for the fire. Each carried her own baby tied on her back.

Strange thing! In the two gospel narratives of the birth at Bethlehem, no woman other than Mary is mentioned. There are men aplenty: the Emperor in Rome, the Governor in Syria, the shepherds, the soldiers, foreign travellers, chief priests and scribes, and a nervous King in Jerusalem. And, of course, Joseph. Sure, Elizabeth was at home in the hill country, and the Widow Anna in the Temple – but no women at a birth?

If common experience and the kindness of people are anything to go by, there would have been lots of women there to help the young mother, so far from her own home and family. There is a tough love women keep for times like this: washing clothes and bathing the infant, boiling water (they're always boiling water at births!), encouraging and bossing Mary, preparing food, joking among themselves, whooshing Joseph out of the way to go make himself useful somewhere else. But Matthew and Luke say nothing of this in their accounts of these events. I know, they had a

A batik from Nigeria depicts a traditional village scene.

different agenda and were more concerned with the meaning of it all, but the women were written out of the story.

However, these women belong in the story: when it all turned horrible, it was their babies, tied on their backs, that Herod ordered his soldiers to kill. The historians of the time did not list that among the many atrocities committed by Herod against his enemies and his own family. Had the women again been written out of the story? But then, history is not usually written about the lives of women, or of the poor in general.

Yet, part of the meaning and the mystery that Matthew and Luke sought in this birth is exactly that: God made this entry into the human story unseen and unnoticed, in an isolated place and among unnamed women. How quickly the battle lines were drawn, and the innocent bystanders cut down! This could be a dirty business; it could all end badly – the signs of the cross were there from the beginning. Even so, it was the women again who were the first to see the Risen Christ and to proclaim the gospel of his resurrection, and ours. And the men were very slow to listen to them (Luke 24:1-12). Do you think that women are still being written out of the story?

(December 2001)

We continue the story of the birth of Jesus, as told in Matthew's Gospel, Chapter 2.

Who Goes There?

When Herod died, an angel of the Lord suddenly appeared in a dream to Joseph in Egypt and said, "Get up, take the child and his mother, and go to the land of Israel, for those who were seeking the child's life are dead." Then Joseph got up, took the child and his mother, and went to the land of Israel. But when he heard that Archelaus was ruling over Judea in place of his father Herod, he was afraid to go there. And after being warned in a dream, he went away to the district of Galilee. There he made his home in a town called Nazareth.
(Matthew 2:19-23)

"What part of Ireland are you from?" It is always a difficult question for me. Because of my father's job, we moved house many times while I was growing up. Indeed, to my child's eye, it sometimes seemed we were in fact moving a house: huge removals vans to carry the furniture, clothing, bedding and books for a family of eight people. (For the curious: he was a school inspector.) It was all fairly benign, and not especially unusual, but it has left me unsure where my home place is.

However, it is not benign, and unfortunately not unusual, for millions of people all over the world in our own time who are forced to move house, except that for them the "house" goes on their heads or on a donkey or a cart. As much or as little as they can carry. Refugees from wars and persecution. Peasants driven off the land they have farmed for generations. Victims of earthquake or famine or flood. Mary and Joseph making a dash for it down the old road to Egypt, in fear for their lives, and their infant son's. People who have lost their place in the world.

There was an extraordinary moment in the summer of 1994 when half a million refugees walked out of Rwanda into Zaire, a river of people fleeing one of the most appalling slaughters of the century. Then, a few weeks later, to the amazement of a watching world, they walked back again: they'd had enough and were going home, to their own place, whatever awaited them there.

The batik from Brazil shows a peasant family driven from their land, with only the barest hope of any kind of life in the city. And yet as I look at it, I see a mirror image: Joseph and Mary with their young son returning from exile in Egypt, now that it is more-or-less safe to do so. Like refugees

On the move: this Brazilian batik captures the plight of a family forced to take what belongings they can carry and set out into the unknown.

anywhere, to find again their place in the world. Or, at the very least, a place that can become their own.

There is a shadow side to the sense of place: when I deny it to others, or do nothing to help them regain their own. When I find in myself, or in my country, a reluctance to welcome the refugee, the stranger, the simply strange. We should know enough about it from our own Irish history and geography: there are marching seasons, and turf wars, and border lines that say, "This is my place, and you may not enter!" I think of the old military challenge: "Who goes there?" And wonder am I afraid what the answer might be.

(January/February 2002)

I try to imagine what it was like for the Holy Family in exile in Egypt. The story is told in Matthew 2:13-23, but in the batik I see Joseph, the Angel, Mary and the child Jesus. I put voices in their mouths, but can only guess what might have been in their minds.

Out of Egypt

"To fulfil what had been spoken by the Lord through the prophet, 'Out of Egypt I have called my son.'"
(Matthew 2:15)

"He looked about my own age, a bit worn from all his travelling, but he was an angel alright. Dreams are funny that way: things are different, unexpected, yet you know what's what. Anyway, he sat down with me – in the dream, you understand – and told me it was time we went home. 'Things have changed for the better,' he said, 'it's safer now.' After all this time they'll have forgotten about us." He looked at the leather bag that contained his livelihood, the tools of an itinerant carpenter. "This is a terrible place; there are no trees here! When we get home, I'll be able to set up a proper workshop." For a long time it had shamed him that he couldn't provide for his family better.

"Home," she thought, "where is that going to be?" For as long as she could remember, it seemed, they had been on the move. First to Bethlehem and the birth; just getting used to things there, when they were off to Egypt. And now, uprooting again, to go back – to whom, to what? She looked at her reflection in the water she was carrying: she still had her girlish good looks, but she had left her girlhood far behind. She had met her own angel, but she wasn't a dreamer like her husband; more a listener. She could hear the words of an ancestor of hers, echoing from centuries away: "Where you go, I will go; Where you lodge, I will lodge; your people shall be my people, and your God my God" (Ruth 1). All that had happened, she knew, had been because of her son; she was learning it would always be that way.

For the boy it was different: Egypt was the only home he had ever really known. He spoke its language well, with a local accent, picking it up from his playmates in the easy way children have; his parents were still struggling with it. For all that he had been born there, the Land of Israel was for him a strange and foreign place – not home. He stood, uneasily watching the adults, and listening to their talk. The tree was a comfort to him – it, at least, was set and sure of its roots. He would miss it, and his other friends, but he was just a child, and in the end would go where he was led. In a sense, it would always be that way for him too. "Out of Egypt I have called my son" (Hosea 11).

This batik from Burkina Faso shows a family and its visitor beside a sturdy tree, which would always be of interest to a carpenter like Joseph, or to those who rarely see forests.

The boy may not have realised it – his father did, as it touched on his trade – but the tree he stood under was a rarity. Egypt has no forests. You have to go farther north for that, for the cedars of Lebanon, the sycamores and the holm oaks and the mastic trees. The kind of solid timber they used for houses and stables and shrines. And for crucifying criminals. The boy would not have known that either.

I'm imagining, of course: what would it have been like for a family in exile, bound up in the long, mysterious unfolding of God's hopes? The batik from Burkina Faso seemed to tell the story. It's true about the trees, though, at least in our own days: I remember an Egyptian friend wandering enthralled through woods and groves of trees on her first visit to Ireland. In her own country, she had never seen more than a solitary tree at a time.

(January/February 2003)

We don't often attend to the lists of ancestors given in Luke 3:23-38 and Matthew 1:1-17, but they can contain some surprises.

Spice Girls for Christmas

An account of the genealogy of Jesus the Messiah, the son of David, the son of Abraham…Tamar…Rahab…Ruth…Bathsheba…Mary.
(Matthew 1:1-16)

I used to think that in the Gospel accounts of the birth of Jesus, Mary was the only woman named; that the other women, who surely would have been there, had been written out of the story.

I had forgotten the genealogies, the lists of the ancestors of Jesus that are given by both Matthew (Chapter 1) and Luke (Chapter 3). In the genealogy given by Matthew, who is in fact mainly concerned with the male ancestry of Jesus back as far as David and Abraham, he names four women – five, if you include Mary his mother. Their stories would make good Christmas reading for you!

Tamar had to fight for her rights, even to playing the role of prostitute to her father-in-law, the patriarch Judah (Genesis 38). Judah himself acted poorly in the whole sordid affair, but at least he had the grace to acknowledge that Tamar "is more in the right than I am." Tamar's son Perez will be an ancestor of David, and so of Jesus.

The David line continues through **Rahab**, who was an actual prostitute in Jericho. Two Israelites who had come to spy out the land of Canaan arrived at her house: she hid them, at mortal risk to herself and her family, and in doing so won life and a lasting remembrance (Joshua 2; Hebrews 11:31; James 2:25. And see *City on Lockdown*, page 96). In Matthew's genealogy she becomes the great-great-grandmother of David.

Ruth was an alien from Moab; she gave up her people, her land, and her faith in a wild chance and followed her Israelite mother-in-law Naomi back to the land of Israel. "Where you go, I will go; where you lodge, I will lodge; your people shall be my people and your God my God." Through some scheming with Naomi, Ruth manages to marry Boaz, and so becomes the great-grandmother of David. (Ruth)

With **Bathsheba**, we meet David directly. He is now king and, simply put, he falls for Bathsheba, a married woman. He arranges the murder

of her husband Uriah, and then takes the widow as his wife. It is not clear how willing a partner she was in all this, or if she had any choice against the will of the king. At any rate, the child of their adultery dies (2 Samuel 11-12), but, much later, Bathsheba fights like a tigress for the right of another son, Solomon, to become king after David (1 Kings Chapters 1 and 2).

What challenges might face the young girl selling fish in this batik from Sri Lanka?

You never know what skeletons you'll uncover in tracing your family tree. The decisive, irregular lives of these four women are like spice to the bland fare we have made of Christmas. Their blood in Jesus' veins reminds us that Bethlehem was not soft and pretty; it was down and dirty, uncertain, even dangerous. Rather like their own lives. As with all who "sit in darkness and in the shadow of death" (Luke 1:79), they had a need for drawing on God's mercy – but they were more valiant than most. In fact, Mary might have welcomed their questionable company; she was a bit unconventional herself, and as an unmarried pregnant woman was already at odds with her own society's values (Matthew 1:18-25; Luke 1:26-56). That's a lonely place to be, as any of the four could have told her.

(December 2004)

9

This article was written over a number of weeks, interweaving the story of the child Jesus with that of an African boy; until I finished it I did not know how it would end, whether the boy would live or die. Writing his story was a way of praying for him.

For the Life of the Boy

Then Simeon blessed them and said to his mother Mary,
'This child is destined for the falling and the rising of many in Israel,
and to be a sign that will be opposed...
and a sword will pierce your own soul too.'
(Luke 2:34-35)

The child was desperately sick; just over a year old, and already slipping away. The parents sent a message: "Father, consider us for the life of the boy."

The journey begins at the moment of conception: *"For it was you who created my being, / knit me together in my mother's womb"* (Psalm 139:13). Life is a high-risk area, whether before birth or after. The innocence of infancy is no protection against the hazards of living: the very instructions for life in our cells may be damaged; or the growing child be harmed by sickness, warfare, famine, sharp objects or blunt instruments, drugs or poisons, rejection, abuse, or a simple lack of loving.

Simeon warned Mary about this, as any parent could have done who had watched over a dying child and been torn to ribbons by the same sword of sorrow (Luke 2:35). She carried her son to safety in Egypt, running before the slaughter (Matthew 2:13-18); but how often did Mary have to keep vigil by his sick bed? Children have to be minded.

When I visited the sick child in the hospital three weeks ago, he cried at the sight of me. They said it wasn't my white face that did it, but my white clothes: everyone who had been sticking needles into him, for injections or IV feeding or blood transfusions, had been dressed in white. How can an infant know that we hurt to heal?

There was a time she lost him and for three days was frantic (Luke 2:41-51). It was little to her that the old men in the Temple were amazed at his wisdom; he was only twelve, too young to be wandering off on his own like that. There are thousands of child soldiers drugged and dragged to be killers at that age – they are lost to their parents; some of them had been made to kill their parents.

"Today in the town of David a saviour has been born to you." (Picture: Vie de Jésus MAFA)

Then the hospital staff went on strike, and the wards were emptied. They brought the boy back home, with what medication and advice and hope they could gather.

I think it is in every sense vital for us that the Son of God had to live a full human life from embryo to adult; that, in the old phrase, "he grew in wisdom, age and grace with God and man" (Luke 2:52). This is what incarnation means, it seems to me: not just what Jesus said or did but what he was, and what – and who – he finally became. But first he had to survive: "My God, the children of the earth / find refuge in the shelter of your wings" (Psalm 36:8). A God who becomes one of "the children of the earth" needs as much minding as any of us.

The boy still lives, nourished and cherished with great care. The figures are not in his favour: the infant mortality rate here is twelve times what it is in Ireland. For some reason that shames me; maybe it should shame us all. But they brought him to Mass this morning, to give thanks for life and love and all that is yet to come. Father, consider us for the life of the boy.

(December 2005)

Here I am imagining, in Elizabeth's voice, how she might have recalled the visit of her cousin Mary while both of them were pregnant. Luke gives his own version of all this in the first chapter of his Gospel. Janet Morley's take on Mary's Magnificat is her poem, "Sing Out, My Soul" – see page 1 for full version.

Visitation

In those days Mary set out and went with haste to a Judean town in the hill country, where she entered the house of Zechariah and greeted Elizabeth.
(Luke 1:5-56)

"I watched her go. Just before the turn that would take her from my sight, she stopped and looked back – then dropped her bag and ran and ran towards me, crashed gasping into my arms. She clung to me till she quieted, then looked at me and brushed the tears from my cheeks, and without a word set off again on the road home. I've never seen anyone so brave, and so frightened – she had no idea what awaited her in Nazareth, or anywhere in the future.

"She had come to us three months earlier, when I felt as big as a wardrobe, and it was so good to see her. I needed her calm good sense, and a bit of cheering up – it was no joke my old frame carrying that weight around all day.

"Then one night, four or five weeks after she arrived, she told me: trying out the sentences, the turns of the story, the drift of her conversation with the angel, laying out the pieces as if to see what pattern they might make. It was the first time she had told anyone she was pregnant, let alone all the rest of it. Maybe she had to wait that time to find out, to be sure. Strangely, I wasn't surprised. I think all surprise had been knocked out of me by my own pregnancy, especially as it wasn't I who had met the angel, but Zechariah. All I had to go on was the lout kicking away inside me!

"There was a song she used to sing that went,
> *Sing out, my soul,*
> *sing of the holiness of God:*
> *who has delighted in a woman…*
Well, we were delighted anyway, though a bit nervous: for both of us a first pregnancy – she young and unmarried, and I ancient. Two fraught conditions! But in the song it is God who is delighted – that should count for something.

"There was the question of Joseph – how would he take it? I liked Joseph; he had stayed with us once on his way to Jerusalem. Solid as oak – the blood runs true there. Of course, I wasn't the one who would have to face him. But then, as Mary said, it goes beyond Joseph or the tongues in the village: if everything the angel said is true, then we're in for it, in a big way, all of us. How was it her song went – *lifted up the poor, satisfied the hungry, given voice to the silent.* We'll never hear the end of it!

"They're all wondering how my John will turn out, but it's Mary's child they'll have to watch for. I've got a feeling of fulfilment about him, a promise being finally settled, as if this was something that God has wanted to do for a long time. I think Mary had the same sense of it: *...who has desired the darkness of the womb, and inhabited our flesh. Sing of the longing of God, sing out, my soul."*

The ink drawing of two women is by Nigerian artist, Agboola Johnson.

(December 2006)

13

This batik from Nigeria made many connections: three men visiting Sarah and Abraham (Genesis 18:1-15), shepherds and magi at Bethlehem, Fulani herdsmen honouring the birth of a child....

Fulani Nativity

In that region there were shepherds living in the fields, keeping watch over their flock by night. Then an angel of the Lord stood before them.
(Luke 2:1-20; see Matthew 2:1-12)

*T*he three men had come to the stable, as the three had come to the tent of Abraham (Genesis 18:1-15). For the Patriarch and his wife Sarah they brought the promise of a son, but Mary's child was already born before her visitors arrived, Fulani herdsmen with their staffs and their cattle. Abraham brought water to wash the travellers' feet, and ran to lay out a meal for them: "curds and milk and the calf he had prepared." But what had Joseph to offer his three guests? Only a drink of cold water, as Fr Joe Purcell my colleague in the parish here pointed out to me when he looked at this batik from Nigeria. It was the hospitality of the poor, and it was sufficient.

Fulani cattle herders do not figure in the Gospel accounts of the birth of Jesus; it was shepherds, not cowboys, who "went with haste and found Mary and Joseph, and the child lying in the manger" (Luke 2:16). But there is an instinct among artists to populate their works with people from their own time and place: popes have appeared in Christmas cribs and paintings, as have street children from São Paulo and rice farmers from China. And a Nigerian artist brought the Fulani to Bethlehem.

Most of the Fulani are nomads and they seem to have had a long history of it. It is thought that they originated in the Middle East and migrated across North Africa to Senegal on the western edge of the continent. From there, about a thousand years ago, they began to make their way eastward again, and now range over the grasslands of several West African countries, among them Nigeria.

Some decades ago, Abuja began to be built, a new city traced across a large tract of land in central Nigeria. It was to replace Lagos as the Capital City. Whatever its effect on the political life of the country, it hasn't as yet made much difference to the nomadic Fulani. I can watch them any day leading their cattle through the housing estate where we live, or threading major intersections in other parts of the city: they let them through the traffic in herds of about thirty or forty at a time – the cattle usually more orderly

Three Fulani herdsmen come to Bethlehem; a batik from Nigeria.

than the motorists. The fact that someone has built a city athwart their traditional pathways has meant only minor detours, not major disruption.

Jesus himself picked up nomadic ways later in his life, and often had "nowhere to lay his head" (Luke 9:58). Rather like the Fulani, who don't see themselves as poor – how could you be poor if you have cattle? – but neither do they carry much excess baggage. In a sense, we too are nomads, belonging to a "pilgrim Church" (Eucharistic Prayer III), and needn't be surprised that we are encouraged to travel lightly. "Take nothing for your journey, no staff, nor bag, nor bread, nor money – not even an extra tunic" (Luke 9:3). That way we might rely more on the hospitality of the poor, as Jesus intended; it is most gracious.

(December 2007)

Surface Area

The bread that we break, is it not a sharing in the body of Christ?
Because there is one bread, we who are many are one body,
for we all partake of the one bread.
(1 Corinthians 10:16-17)

Consider your lungs: two sponges, each with an air system and a blood system that divide and subdivide and intertwine until air and blood almost touch each other – only a cell-width separates them. That's where the vital exchange takes place: oxygen from air to blood and into your body, and carbon dioxide out from blood to air where it is breathed away. If you could spread out all the tiny places and surfaces where this exchange takes place in human lungs, it would be about the size of a tennis court. That's a large effective area for gas exchange, every breath you take.

Surface area is crucial in nature and in the mechanics of our living. The grills on the radiators in our cars or in our home central heating provide more surface area, the better to transfer heat – either to get rid of it or to warm our houses. The bristles on a brush, the tufts on a towel, the spray from a shower rose or a watering can – more surface area, more active contact. Even the clouds of pollen and seeds spreading life (and irritation!) in our atmosphere: sessile plants enlarging their surface area, connecting with other plants or searching for fertile growing places.

Could this be Christmas language, Jesus being God's surface area in our tangible world? God with skin on, as someone put it, so as to touch people, lay hands on them, embrace them. It's where the vital exchange takes place. *"She said, 'If I but touch his clothes, I will be made well'"* (Mark 5:28, and 5:41, 7:33, 8:23). At Bethlehem Jesus himself had to be touched, washed with water and rubbed with oil and ointment, as might the skin of any baby. Or the skin of a dead body taken from a cross (Mark 16:1; John 19:40). This is indeed Christmas language, and more!

Perhaps twenty-five years after Calvary, St Paul wrote to the church of Corinth: *"Now you are the body of Christ and individually members of it"* (1 Corinthians 12:27). It was a thing he insisted on, that Christ has risen from death, and now the Church – the body of believers – was his presence to the

Details:
Adire cloth
from Nigeria.

world. The surface area of Christ, where the vital exchange takes place. That can be hard to believe when we look at the often sordid history of the Church, or at ourselves in all our weakness and failure. But then, Jesus of Nazareth was familiar with weakness and failure.

For the poet Gerard Manley Hopkins, the surface area of Christ in the world is a playground: "for Christ plays in ten thousand places, / Lovely in limbs, and lovely in eyes not his / To the Father through the features of men's faces" (*As Kingfishers Catch Fire*). I sometimes wonder why Church news is so often dispiriting and contentious, when there could be so much tangible joy in it: a mother delighting in the limbs and eyes of her adorable baby; the bread and wine and water and oil of our sacraments; the glorious companionship of a God with skin on. "And the Word became flesh and lived among us." (John 1:14)

(December 2008)

17

This is an imagination-piece: what were the thoughts of Matthew the Gospel writer as he tries to tell the story of the birth of Jesus. His is a Jewish mindset: for answers to his questions, he searches the scriptures!

The Gospel Writer

In the time of King Herod, after Jesus was born in Bethlehem, wise men from the East came to Jerusalem…
(Matthew, Chapter 2)

"I have with me a copy of what Mark has written, but as you know I am trying to write something myself. I've been gathering all the information I can, to add to what Mark has, and of course he has nothing at all about the birth of Jesus, or his childhood. So I've been asking around, especially among older people coming from Jerusalem and the Bethlehem area, since we know Jesus was born there. There's the chance that someone might remember something, some family story handed down. But there's very little; it may be just too long ago, about eighty years now since the time of Herod the Great.

"As it happens, one of the few stories I did come across involves the same Herod. It's about some strangers who came to Bethlehem one night – no one was sure who they were; *magi* possibly, being from the East. Anyway, it seems they had been blundering about Jerusalem asking where they could find the 'new-born King of the Jews', as they put it. Totally unaware of how dangerous that was! They had seen signs in the heavens, they said, and there was an unusual star. It all alarmed King Herod, who saw plots against himself around every corner, and it terrified everyone else.

"Herod sent them on to Bethlehem; that was where the prophet Micah had said a new ruler would come from. There the strangers visited one family who did indeed have a baby boy. But by the next morning they were gone: foreigners, parents, baby and all. Perhaps they had been warned – but who could have done that? The family fled to Egypt; nobody knew where the foreigners went. It would all have been forgotten except for its terrible outcome, the revenge taken by Herod on the infant boys of Bethlehem: he had his soldiers kill them all. It was my first time hearing of that atrocity.

"Now, what do I do with this? Is it part of the story of Jesus? Or is it about someone else? Or is there any truth in it? As always seems to happen, the very people who could have told me are gone – Mary and Joseph! And yet, my Jewish instincts rise to the tale; it is full of echoes from our past. The *magi* search the skies; but we search the scriptures.

Although the Bible does not say the eastern strangers were kings, long tradition says they were, and that is how Anne Murphy, an Irish artist, has portrayed them. (©Anne Murphy, *Eala Enamels*)

"Take the very name 'Joseph' – there was an earlier Joseph, a great man for dreams, son of the Patriarch Jacob and Rachel; he went down to Egypt and ended up saving his family. Centuries later, a ruler in Egypt ordered the death of all Hebrew boys, but Moses escaped that slaughter, and became another saviour of the Jewish people. Still with the death of children, I can hear the prophet Jeremiah's words about Rachel, who is buried near Bethlehem: 'weeping for her children, because they are no more'. And then, what the Lord said through the prophet Hosea: 'When Israel was a child, I loved him, / and out of Egypt I called my son.' Are these echoes of a deeper truth? How can I tell this story?"

*If you want to know what the gospel writer did with the story, read Matthew, Chapter 2. For the words of Hosea see Hosea 11:1, and for Rachel's lament, Jeremiah 31:10-17. And for Rachel again read, **Refusing to be comforted**, page 80.*

(January/February 2009)

The evangelist Luke weaves the words of Isaiah into his account of the shepherds at the birth of Jesus. (Luke 2:8-20)

The Sign

This will be a sign for you: you will find a child wrapped in bands of cloth and lying in a manger.
(Luke 2:12)

First, the angel gave the shepherds a sign, then they broke into song: *Glory to God in the highest heaven, and on earth peace among those whom he favours* (Luke 2:14). But these Jewish shepherds already had a sign, one that was centuries old and from the great prophet Isaiah: *Therefore the Lord himself will give you a sign. Look, the young woman is with child and shall bear a son, and shall name him Immanuel* (Isaiah 7:10-17). And Isaiah too begins to sing:

> *For a child has been born for us,*
> *a son given to us;*
> *authority rests upon his shoulders;*
> *and he is named*
> *Wonderful Counsellor, Mighty God,*
> *Everlasting Father, Prince of Peace.*
> (Isaiah 9:6)

Most likely, this song comes from the coronation ceremony of a new king. A king in Jerusalem – any king – was literally a Messiah, a Christ: the words (from Hebrew and Greek) mean 'anointed'. It was by being anointed that kings were "crowned" since the time of Saul and David, to become the *"Lord's Anointed"* (I Samuel 10:1; 24:1-7; II Samuel 2:4). The angel's message to the shepherds also refers to the Lord's Anointed: "*I am bringing you good news of great joy for all the people: to you is born this day in the city of David a Saviour, who is the Messiah, the Lord*" (Luke 2:10-11).

The shepherds rushed off to see for themselves, *"and found Mary and Joseph, and the child lying in a manger"* (Luke 2:16). Afterwards, on the way back from Bethlehem, the shepherds sang: it was all just as they had been told – not only by the angel, but in the Book of Isaiah. In this way the evangelist Luke tells the story of the birth of Jesus.

Christmas for many has become a mid-winter Festival of Lights, with shopping attached. Stores and supermarkets hope it will make up for poor sales earlier in the year. True, there is the giving of gifts at Christmas, which

Christmas card from Rwanda, handmade from banana leaves.

is near to the heart of the matter. But many Christmas cards no longer name the event, and dare no more than "Season's Greetings" or "Happy Holiday!" And there have even been objections to Nativity cribs erected in public places. That would be a loss. For where the teaching has failed, and the scriptures are unknown, and a new "religious illiteracy" is abroad, it may fall to the crib to carry the Christmas story. Whether anyone will believe in the story is, of course, another question, but at least they'll have heard of it.

For there's not much meaning to Christmas if it does not involve a baby, a completed mother, and a proud father: who was it said, *"This is my Son, my Beloved; listen to him"?* (Luke 9:28-36).

(December 2009)

21

This reflection is inspired by two songs: the Song of Simeon, Nunc Dimittis, *in Luke's account of the Presentation of Jesus in the Temple (Luke 2:22-38), and an old song from the Irish tradition,* Caoineadh na dTrí Mhuire.

Three for a Girl

At last, all-powerful Master,
you give leave to your servant
to go in peace, according to your promise.
For my eyes have seen your salvation
which you have prepared for all nations,
the light to enlighten the Gentiles
and give glory to your people Israel.
(*Song of Simeon Luke 2:29-32,* Grail)

W ere Simeon in any way like me he'd have held that baby with great trepidation, not because it was the light of the world he was holding, but because babies a few weeks old are breakable – or so it seems to me. Whenever I am given one to hold and bless, I'm terrified I'll drop it, or damage it in some way, and I hand it back to its mother as soon as I decently can.

But, in the event, it was the grown man who was breakable; the song of Simeon was matched by another, from the Irish tradition: *Caoineadh na dTrí Mhuire*, the Lament of the Three Marys.

> *Can this be the little Son I carried for three seasons?*
> > *Ochón and Ochón O!*
> *Or is this the little Son that was born in the stable?*
> > *Ochón and Ochón O!*
> *Or is this the little Son that was reared at Mary's breast?*
> > *Ochón and Ochón O!*

All but one of the men had fled. But there were some women who stayed – they stood either at a distance or right beside the cross, and after the death they prepared to anoint the broken body. In particular it seems from the tradition that there were three Marys on Calvary that day: Mary "the mother" (as John calls her), Mary Magdalene, and a third Mary remembered variously as mother of James or wife of Clopas (Mark 15:40; Matthew 27:56; Luke 23:55; 24:10; John 19:25-26). They form the background to this old Irish poem, or at least to its title: usually only the voice of "the mother" is heard in the lament. In one version, she calls the other two Marys to draw near "to mourn my shining love."

22

"Unity Mask" by Nigerian artist M Oladoja.

Simeon was aware of the divisive potential of the child he was holding, and he warned Mary she could be caught in a backlash against her son. Running through the Gospels there is a thread of unease between Jesus and those closest to him – his own family, his neighbours in the village, and even some of his chosen followers and friends. On Calvary's cross Mary witnessed the climax of that contradiction; Simeon called it a sword that would break her heart. And the two Marys reply, "What have we to mourn over unless we mourn his bones?"

When Simeon speaks to Mary his voice is heavy with the darkness over Calvary (Luke 1:33-35; 23:44), but when he sings, it is brightness – more a shout than a song! The child in his arms is "the light to enlighten the Gentiles", crashing into creation from the beginning of all: *"Then God said, 'Let there be light'; and there was light"* (Genesis 1:3). Or as John put it, *"The true light, which enlightens everyone, was coming into the world"* (John 1:9). And Mary the mother, watching the darkness settle about the body of her son, calls him *"mo ghrá geal"*, my bright and shining love.

(December 2010)

23

From the Middle East of three thousand years ago, to Germany two centuries ago, to our own time and place, this is a Christmas story: children are precious and need to be protected.

House of Bread

But you, O Bethlehem of Ephrathah,
        who are one of the little clans of Judah,
        from you shall come forth for me
        one who is to rule in Israel....
        And he shall stand and feed his flock
in the strength of the Lord.
(Micah 5:2-4; see Matthew 2:1-6)

This is a tale of two houses, one of them being Bethlehem in Judah. Naomi, together with her husband and their two sons, fled from Bethlehem at a time of famine, to find food in the land of Moab. Ten years later, after the deaths of her husband and both her sons, Naomi returns home with Ruth her daughter-in-law, just as barley is about to be harvested. The famine is over: Bethlehem – the name means "House of Bread", a granary – is once again a place of nourishment.

Bethlehem is also a place of birth. Ruth is courted by a kind and wealthy land-owner called Boaz – *"Come here, and eat some of this bread, and dip your morsel in the sour wine"* (Ruth 2:14) – and they marry and have a son, whom they name Obed. Two generations later, still at Bethlehem, their great-grandson is born: David, who will be King in Jerusalem. (For all this, see the Book of **Ruth**.)

A thousand years later, *"Jesus Christ, the son of David...was born in Bethlehem of Judea in the days of Herod the king"* (Matthew 1 - 2). Naomi's story has run its course: in the House of Bread, God is with us as a child.

There is another house, not set in the Scriptures but among the stories gathered in Germany two hundred years ago by Jacob and Wilhelm Grimm. Two children, Hansel and Gretel, are trapped by an evil witch who eats human flesh and has built a house of the sweetest foods imaginable – just the kind of place to tempt a child to enter: a gingerbread house. The children escape, of course, but there remains a sense of danger and deception, where the weak are threatened, where children are enticed and their lives destroyed.

Two houses, and we might find ourselves in either of them – as Jesus did, and barely escaped, when Herod *"sent and killed all the male children in Bethlehem and in all that region who were two years old or under"* (Matthew 2:16). Even in the House of Bread the child needs to be protected.

But Jesus survived, to "stand and feed his flock in the strength of the Lord," as the prophet Micah foretold of him – he gave bread to thousands! (Mark 6:30-44). In the end, he gave himself: *"And as they were eating, he took*

Pen and ink drawing from Nigeria

bread, and blessed, and broke it, and gave it to them, and said, 'Take; this is my body'" (Mark 14:22). It is a thing any good shepherd would do; as Jesus said to Peter: *"Feed my sheep"* (John 21:15-17). It is what the Church must do.

And so to our own days: *"Let the children come to me, do not hinder them; for to such belongs the kingdom of God"* (Mark 10:13-16). I think what arouses the greatest anger are the times when the Church fails in this, and then behaves no differently from any other organisation protecting its own interests. It is an old instinct to defend your own; we could, any of us, find within ourselves the same tendency and temptation. We need to remember which kind of House we are called to build: a House of Bread, where all find welcome, nourishment, protection and love – and the bread of life (John 6:25-35).

(December 2011)

2: Psalms

The praises of Israel

A very brief introduction to the psalms, though I cannot supply the music that should go with them.

Soul Music

It is good to give thanks to the Lord,
to make music to your name, O Most High,
to proclaim your love in the morning
and your truth in the watches of the night,
On the ten-stringed lyre and the lute,
with the murmuring sound of the harp.
(Psalm 92)

Imagine what it would be like if we said, but did not sing, "For he's a jolly good fellow," or "Happy Birthday to You!" If the Liverpool fans did not sing, but simply stood up and recited their anthem, "You'll never walk alone"? I think something would be missing. Why do we sing? For the fun of it, for the beauty of it, but also, I think, to reach beyond the saying power of words only.

As prayers go, the psalms are marathon-runners: some of them almost three thousand years old. Some are casual, personal, even intimate; others are more formal, crafted by poets; and still others give the impression they are bits and pieces, remnants of long liturgical services. What they all have in common is that originally they would have been put to music; that's the way it was – praise wasn't only spoken, it was sung: *"I will sing forever of your love, O Lord"* (Psalm 89). Now, of course, the words are still there, but the music is long gone – to turn the phrase, the melody didn't linger on.

The great King David in Jerusalem was a noted musician – his playing on the harp soothed the ragged nerves of his predecessor Saul on a few occasions (1 Samuel 16:14-23) – and he probably composed psalms himself. So it is no surprise that, much later when the various psalms were being gathered together in small collections like hymn books, some of them were attributed to David, and even attached to episodes in his life. Psalm 51 has a heading: *"A Psalm of David, when the prophet Nathan came to him, after he had gone in to Bathsheba"* (see 2 Samuel 11:1 – 12:15). All of this would have given the psalms an added acceptability, you might say. In the end, it was recognised that these prayers, which had come from so many different people and circumstances, were inspired and contained the Word of God: they became part of the sacred writings of the Hebrew scriptures, part of the Bible.

In 1997 at the funeral of Princess Diana, Elton John sang one of his own songs, *Candle in the Wind*. It captured the grief of a nation. It had originally been written in 1973 about Marilyn Monroe, and only later adapted for Diana. I suppose there was a similar sadness in the two

This batik depicts an old harpist from Cameroon in West Africa. The wisdom of many traditions has been passed on in song and story.

stories. This kind of thing has happened with the psalms too: they could be written for one occasion, but later made to serve another purpose. They are Jewish songs, but we have adopted them as our prayer, and the prayer of the Church.

Pity about the music, though. I live in Africa, among a people who freely sing when praying; it's something that I, like many an Irishman, cannot easily do. Yet, it's not just about being Irish – maybe I don't have enough fire in my soul about God and God's world to break out in song. Perhaps there is something I could learn from the Liverpool fans.

(May 2002)

Psalm 1 sets the tone for the entire collection, the Praises of Israel: we can choose life or death, goodness or evil. And yet the choices we face in our lives may not always be so clear or so simple.

At least be hypocrites!

Happy indeed are those
who follow not the counsel of the wicked,
nor linger in the way of sinners
nor sit in the company of scorners,
but whose delight is the law of the Lord
and who ponder his law day and night.

They are like a tree that is planted
beside the flowing waters,
that yields its fruit in due season
and whose leaves shall never fade;
and all that they do shall prosper.
Not so are the wicked, not so!
For they like winnowed chaff
shall be driven away by the wind.
(Psalm 1)

The desert teaches a hard lesson: without water you die. This is the reality behind the first psalm and its sharp contrast of life and death, good and evil. Beside the flowing waters the good stand tall and strong. "Not so the wicked, not so!" They are scattered like dust, already dead. It is a stark, simple view of things.

The psalm poses the question: where do I stand – with the Good, or with the Bad? And what of the Church I belong to? We have become much more aware recently that within the Church there is good and bad, and sometimes very ugly.

And yet we have a message to proclaim and a witness to give, though we have not made that any easier for ourselves. I am in the company of Moses, who was afraid, and Jonah, who ran away, and Peter, who denied his friend, and Judas the betrayer, and Paul, who found he couldn't even do the good he wanted to do. Poor enough messengers. As the same Paul puts it: "We have this treasure in clay jars" – shabby, unworthy, easily broken (2 Corinthians 4:7).

Tree of Life: a batik from The Gambia. The Tree of Life is a powerful symbol of being well-rooted, drawing nourishment that gives growth and bears fruit.

The Bible is hard on hypocrites; Jesus generally had little time for them. Hypocrisy is a rotten thing to be accused of. And yet, I find myself agreeing with a friend of mine: he used to say of us ministers of the gospel: "Let us at least be hypocrites!" Times have changed, and it is a long fall from hero to hypocrite; but however we are perceived, I think we should at least try to act the part – for fear we would lose our nerve entirely, and what needs saying never be said.

Again the desert and the first Psalm: along old, dried-up river beds you will often see a ribbon development of vegetation – the trees have deepened their roots, and are tapping the moisture hidden beneath the arid surface. I think our own roots have been too shallow for too long.

(June 2001)

Perhaps the most popular psalm, but there is a more deadly side to it. Even so, we do not journey alone nor without guidance.

The Darkest Valley

Even though I walk through the darkest valley,
I fear no evil;
For you are with me.
(Psalm 23 NRSV)

We were hiking down the valley of the Wadi Qelt, a river that runs from Jerusalem to Jericho, and most likely the ancient roadway between those two towns. A ragged valley, bone-dry for half the year, it was seen as a dangerous place with armed robbers, beaten victims, and the odd "good Samaritan" (Luke 10:30-37).

At one point we were overtaken by a flash-flood of sheep led by their shepherd, and we thought of Psalm 23: "he leads me beside still waters" (NRSV) – though on this occasion there was no water, and the flock poured to the other side across a dry riverbed. That was when this picture was taken, in December 2003, by one of our sabbatical group in the Holy Land.

Psalm 23, *The Lord is my Shepherd,* is probably the best known of all the psalms, and is certainly the favourite for weddings and First Holy Communions and other happy times. Sweet Music! But not if you consider the fate of sheep. In biblical times, as in our own, sheep were food: lamb chops, roast mutton, Shepherd's Pie…

That is the dark secret at the heart of this psalm: for what purpose do shepherds mind their flocks, leading them to green pastures where they can eat, and drink water, and feel safe? Sheep and lambs were eaten or were offered in sacrifice. Table or Altar: either way we see the "gentle lamb led to the slaughter" (Jeremiah 11:19). I am not trying to spoil the psalm for you! Sweet Music it is, but sweetness and light it is not.

Jesus called himself the Good Shepherd who "lays down his life for the sheep" (John 10:11), yet he knew, as shepherds must, that all his flock would nonetheless die. He knew where the "right paths" led: not just along the contour tracks on the hillsides where the flock could walk easily and safely, but down to the floor of *"the valley of the shadow of death"* as the old translation had it. It was the path he himself walked, knowing well where it went: "Was it not necessary that the Christ should suffer these things and then enter into his glory?" (Luke 24:26). And he asks us to follow him.

Shepherd and his sheep in the Wadi Qelt. (Photo: courtesy D Connolly)

It was written centuries before Jesus lived, yet it seems to me that Psalm 23 captures the essence of his death, that it was not only *for* us, but *with* us. Watch the pronouns! At the very entry to the darkest valley the psalm changes – from speaking *about* the shepherd (verses 1-3), it begins speaking *to* him: *"though I walk through the darkest valley....you are with me!" You* prepare a table, *you* anoint my head (verses 4-5).

At that moment and in that place of darkness, diminishment and death, we recognise the Shepherd. He too was under a death sentence, as John the Baptist knew when he called him the "Lamb of God" (John 1:35-36). It seems we traverse the darkest valley together.

(July/August 2008)

To pray a psalm

The Lord is my light and my help;
whom shall I fear?
(Psalm 27)

A sign I saw in a shop window last Summer. SHOES: SPECIAL OFFER – BUY ONE, GET ONE FREE! Generous of them, I thought. But not unlike Psalm 27: is it one psalm, or have two psalms been run together? Are we getting one free?

As we have it now, the psalm splits easily into two parts, verses 1-6, and 7-14. The singer wants to be near God in the Temple in Jerusalem – to go on pilgrimage, to journey towards God (Psalm 27:1-6):

> *There is one thing I ask of the Lord,*
> *for this I long,*
> *to live in the house of the Lord,*
> *all the days of my life.*

It is a longing born out of a life full of threats and troubles: For there he keeps me safe in his tent / in the day of evil. A longing we might all share, not just for peace and quiet, but for *"the sweetness of the Lord"*, God's beauty and charm.

Then the psalmist states, *I will sing and make music for the Lord* – and quite suddenly the character of the psalm seems to change, and there is a new song (Psalm 27:7-14):

> *O Lord, hear my voice when I call;*
> *have mercy and answer.*
> *Of you my heart has spoken:*
> *"Seek his face."*
> *It is your face, O Lord, that I seek;*
> *hide not your face.*

Psalms have a life of their own and, as we saw with Psalm 23, it is a good tactic in reading one to watch the pronouns. In the first part of Psalm 27 the pronouns are in the third person, *about* God, referring to God. But in the second part, the singer addresses God directly and intimately: you, your. The longing is to see God's face, to look into the eyes of God. It is a dangerous desire; there was a long tradition in the scriptures that no one could see the face of God and live (Genesis 32:30; Exodus 33:20). And it is still dangerous: it means taking God seriously, allowing the Lord to invade my life. The psalmist is very daring, and knows it: *Dismiss not your servant in anger.* As in our Mass: "we have the courage to say, Our Father…"

How would you pray with such a psalm? Again I suggest, watch the pronouns! Sometimes a psalm will say something *to* us, as when the first half of Psalm 27 teaches us about God and our pilgrimage of life. Our longing is to see God's beauty – a longing at the heart of our worship, our Eucharist, our *"sacrifice of joy"*. My way of prayer might be to listen: what is this psalm saying to me?

And sometimes a psalm may speak *for* us, much as a tongue-tied lover might borrow a poet's words: "How do I love thee? Let me count the ways." So I go along with the psalm, follow its lead, let it speak for me; perhaps it will give me courage to say things I might not otherwise dare to say. In the end, it is the Spirit who speaks *to* us and *for* us, whenever we use the psalms in our prayer: "When we cry 'Abba! Father!' it is that very Spirit bearing witness with our spirit..." (see Romans 8:15-16, 26-27).

So, did we get one free? I like to think so, but then I think we get all of them free.

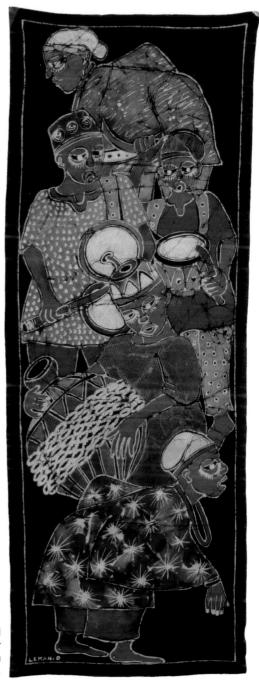

Drummers, singers and dancers make music for the Lord in this batik from Nigeria, West Africa.

(June 2007)

33

In the Liturgy of the Hours, Psalm 88 is said for Night Prayer every Friday – it is the most grief-laden psalm of all.

One for Sorrow

As for me, Lord, I call to you for help;
In the morning my prayer comes before you.
Lord, why do you reject me?
Why do you hide your face?
Wretched, close to death from my youth,
I have borne your trials; I am numb.
(Psalm 88)

I take the title from an old rhyme, a piece of folklore which predicts your future by counting birds: "One for sorrow, two for joy, three for a girl, four for a boy…" Because if ever there is one for sorrow, it is Psalm 88.

There are many psalms of sorrow in the Bible and typically they show a movement from grief and suffering to praise and thanksgiving – after all, that is the purpose of praying them, to find some hope in a time of horror. So, *"Out of the depths I cry to you, O Lord"* leads to the hope that *"with the Lord there is mercy and fullness of redemption"* (Psalm 130:1). Or as Psalm 116:6 puts it, *"The Lord protects the simple hearts / I was helpless so God saved me."* Now that is as pithy as a piece of folklore or an advertising jingle – and as slippery with the truth. Because, as the singer of Psalm 88 – or your own experience – would tell you, things are not always so simple.

There is no happy ending, no hope, in Psalm 88. It opens with a call for help by day and ends, *my one companion is darkness*. God has left me. *And I am like those you remember no more / cut off, as they are, from your hand. / You have laid me in the depths of the tomb, / in places that are dark, in the depths.* No movement, no escape, just playing and replaying the tapes of despair.

God is my enemy, and has taken away my friends. And yet, the singer deeply longs for God. In a sense, this is a most intimate psalm; it is all I/me/my and you/your through thirty-three of its thirty-six lines. This is intense conversation, passionate dialogue – except that it is entirely one-sided. God is silent. No one replies. One hand clapping.

Great grief can rip away our securities. Our most basic beliefs, the things we were sure of and took for granted, crack along faultlines we never knew existed. Especially our beliefs about God. We find that God is not as we thought, or as we had been told. So when a child dies horribly, or my heart breaks for sheer hurt, or endless thousands are killed by a natural disaster, I round on the One who could have done something but didn't. *Your anger weighs down upon me / I am drowned beneath your waves.*

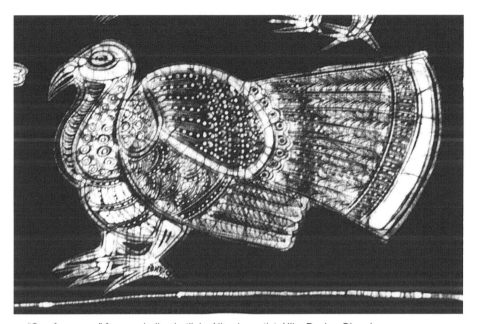

"One for sorrow" from an indigo batik by Nigerian artist, Nike Davies-Okundaye.

If I am to be faithful to the psalm, I must leave it at that and not tack on a happy ending. I may have to sit awhile with the questions it asks: *Lord, why do you reject me? / Why do you hide your face?* Or the question that Jesus asked on Calvary, *"My God, my God, why have you forsaken me?"* (Psalm 22; Matthew 27:46). What more could be said?

(September/October 2005)

A Song, from the wedding of a King and his Princess Bride. Probably especially written for the occasion by a professional poet.

Two For Joy

She is led to the king with her maiden companions.
They are escorted amid gladness and joy;
they pass within the palace of the king.
(Psalm 45)

Think Prince and Princess and happy ever after, and you have the background of Psalm 45. A royal wedding song: which king is not certain, nor who the bride, but in any case their beauty and majesty are honoured. Nor is the heart of the matter forgotten – whatever about fairy-tale romance, royal weddings usually have a very practical purpose: *Sons shall be yours in place of your fathers; / you will make them princes over all the earth.* A song that was sung at the wedding of a king in Israel: *God, your God, has anointed you / with the oil of gladness above other kings.*

But there may be a deeper resonance to Psalm 45. It falls across one of the songlines of the scriptures, one of those great insights that wend their way through the Bible: that God is to his people as a man to his bride.

For your Maker is your husband,
the Lord of hosts is his name…
For the Lord has called you
like a wife forsaken and grieved in spirit…
(Isaiah 54:4-8)

In reaching for ways to describe the closeness and care of God for us, the prophets suggest that God married us: "*I will take you for my wife forever; I will take you for my wife in righteousness and in justice, in steadfast love and in mercy*" (Hosea 2:16-20).

It is an insight rooted in the beginning of things: *Therefore a man leaves his father and his mother and clings to his wife, and they become one flesh* (Genesis 2:24). Of Adam and Eve, and of man and woman, but also of God and us – "they become one flesh". This is strong language! And it flowers in the Christian gospel: *This is a great mystery, and I am applying it to Christ and the church* (Ephesians 5:32). The image of the Church, the Bride of Christ, has had a long history in Christian writing and prayer.

Of course, all this begs the question: how is it, in fact, between men and women in our world? If you are a woman you are far more likely to be beaten, raped, abused or enslaved – or simply disregarded. It may be that men will make decisions about your life, what you may wear, where you may go, whether you will be educated, whether you will live. A woman caught in an abusive marriage may have difficulty with the notion of God as husband to his people.

The ancient wisdom is that a man *leaves his father and his mother and clings to his wife*. What else must he leave? What male bias in his family or his own character? What prejudices in his culture or his religion? Even Psalm 45 betrays a male bias! Yet I believe that praying it may teach me the healing that is needed in my own heart, and in the hearts of mankind.

"Two for Joy", batik by the Nigerian artist, Lekan O.

(July/August 2007)

*Written just after the Tsunami in Japan, 2011. Psalm 109 is a difficult psalm, one of several filled with a desire for vengeance. (See also **Harmattan**, page 164.)*

seeking the ruins

**Let their children lose father and mother
and their spouses know bereavement.
Let their children be wanderers and beggars
driven from the ruins of their home.**
(Psalm 109: 9-10)

The tall grass has withered down about the church at Chika in Nigeria, and the ruined walls of demolished houses are beginning to reappear all around us: we worship in a ghost town. Some years ago, in the Holy Land, I saw fences made of living cactus, hardy growths that had been planted as boundaries to farms and orchards that are now lost or abandoned; their former owners were driven out, but the cactus remains. As I write, in Japan landscapes of human habitations have been destroyed and emptied of people. Clearances, war, earthquake, tsunami – you wouldn't wish it on your worst enemy! But Psalm 109 would.

With the psalms there is always a danger of cherry-picking, of choosing only those that attract and help us. The well-crafted ones, the sweet ones, the cherries. Of course we have our favourites, but many psalms are difficult, and some leave a sour taste: they have a bitter heart, savage and vengeful. Such as Psalms 58 or 83 or 109, and some verses in otherwise blameless songs: "*I hate them with a perfect hate / and they are foes to me*" (Psalm 139:22).

To be evicted from your home is to be mortally wounded. Psalm 109 says more. The original Hebrew does not speak of being 'driven from the ruins', but of *seeking the ruins*: picking through the rubble for shards of a life; recognising the cactus fences of what was once your land – the cactus thrives, but the land is beyond your reach; "searching for houses that exist only in the memory" as Alan Johnston said in a BBC report from Japan, March 20th, 2011. That's a corrosive condition to be in, or to wish upon others: "wanderers and beggars seeking the ruins of their home."

> *Let no one show them mercy
> nor pity their orphaned children.
> Let their sons and daughters be destroyed
> and with them their names be blotted out.*
> (Psalm 109:12-13)

How can such words and sentiments be part of our prayer? In the reforms after the Second Vatican Council, these "cursing" psalms and verses were eliminated from the liturgy. Some didn't agree with that, but it was one way of dealing with the problem – particularly as we were now celebrating the Eucharist and the Liturgy of the Hours in our own languages.

But whatever about our liturgy, these prayers remain part of the inspired word of God in the Bible. What good are they? What caused them to be sung, written down, preserved, gathered into the Sacred Scriptures? Maybe it was out of a sense of honesty: the people who composed and collected the Praises of Israel knew well what we are like. For all our sweet prayers, at times we are vindictive, hateful, unforgiving. We are capable of doing terrible things to other people. And we bend and shape God to our own wishes, to justify what we do.

Forgiveness is not an easy matter, and even the search for justice takes its toll of us. It seems to me these "cursing" psalms are a mirror in which

Ink drawing from Nigeria.

we may recognise some features of our own faces and how adversity has affected us. Such a recognition is a step on the way of healing. Oppressor and oppressed, we need the mercy and the justice of God.

(June 2011)

39

The "Final Solution" of the Holocaust in the 20th Century was not the first time that an attempt was made to destroy the Jewish people; this psalm speaks of an earlier threat.

Final Solution

Shame and terror be theirs for ever;
let them be disgraced, let them perish!
Let them know that your name is the LORD,
the Most High over all the earth.
(Psalm 83:18-19)

The Catholic liturgy excludes Psalm 83 as one of the "cursing" psalms, but in the Bible it is a prayer: *"O God, do not keep silent, / do not be mute and unmoved, O God"* (Psalm 83:1). But what if it were also meant to be heard by the enemy – a piece of wartime propaganda?
As fire that burns away the forest,
as the flame that sets the mountains ablaze,
drive them away with your tempest
and fill them with terror at your storm.
(Psalm 83:15-16)
The God of Israel was noted for burning mountains (Exodus 19:18-25; Psalm 144:5-6). And setting the heather blazing was an old way of rousing the troops and frightening the invaders.

The old enemies are listed – Edom, Moab, Amalek, Philistia, Assyria – and famous victories are invoked, to stiffen the spines of the defenders:
Treat them like Midian, like Sisera,
like Jabin at the River Kishon,
the men who were destroyed at Endor,
whose bodies rotted on the ground.
(Psalm 83:10-11)
There are no half-measures here, no room for mercy or finer shades of meaning. Wartime propaganda tends to be simplistic and extreme.

The background to this psalm is not only war, but genocide: *"They say: 'Come, let us destroy them as a nation; / let the name of Israel be forgotten'"* (Psalm 83:5). It may not have been the first attempt, and certainly was not the last: the 20th century witnessed a spectacular assault on the very existence of the Children of Israel – the Final Solution.

In human history, there have been other massacres and disappearances and extinctions; one way or another, every continent has had its killing fields. And it would seem the more humanity develops, the more powerful

"Cover their faces with shame." (Psalm 83:18) Batik of a mask from Nigeria.

become the means of destroying whole populations. Small wonder Psalm 83 makes its own harsh protest against that prospect: *"My God, scatter them like chaff, / drive them like straw in the wind!"* (Psalm 83:14).

This is an ancient question that Psalm 83 is asking: isn't God on our side, are we not God's people, don't we bless the armies? And yet –
They plot against your people,
conspire against those you love….
they make common alliance against you.
(Psalm 83:4,6)
And God remains silent, mute, unmoved.

On Calvary, as he was being done to death by his own enemies, Jesus protested out of another psalm: *"My God, my God, why have you forsaken me?"* (Psalm 22:1; Matthew 27:46). But God was silent there too.

(July/August 2011)

Psalm 104 celebrates the wonders of Creation, which can be seen in the stars and in the creatures in habitats of air or rock or forest.

The Elephant in the Tree

When Saul returned from following the Philistines, he was told, "David is in the wilderness of En-gedi." Then Saul took three thousand chosen men out of all Israel, and went to look for David and his men in the direction of the Rocks of the Wild Goats.
(I Samuel 24:1-2)

Cousins don't have to look alike. The "Handsome Connollys" swing from a different branch of the family tree – or so I'm told. The mammal in the tree in this picture is a rock badger, a **Hyrax**, but it is indeed a close cousin of the better-known, and much larger, elephant. I took the photograph a few years ago in the Holy Land, at En-gedi – an oasis beside the Dead Sea.

En-gedi is a home for the Hyrax. The Book of Proverbs lists the rock badgers (with ants, locusts and lizards) among things on earth that are small, and yet "are exceedingly wise." *The badgers are a people without power, yet they make their homes in the rocks* (Proverbs 30:24-28). Though that never saved them from being hunted for their meat and their hides.

Also among the fauna at En-gedi are the Wild Goats, the **Ibex**; they too are sure-footed on the rocks and the cliffs. And, like the Hyrax, there was a time when they had been hunted almost to extinction. Only a Wild Animal Protection Law enacted in 1955 prevented that happening. It is as well – both animals have been around a long time, and are named in Psalm 104, a song that was composed about two and a half thousand years ago:

> *The high mountains are for the wild goats;*
> *the rocks are a refuge for the badgers.*
> (104:18 RSV)

Psalm 104 follows much the same sequence as the accounts of creation in the Book of Genesis; it celebrates the harmonies of light and life, water and sky, humus and humanity. It rejoices in the rhythms of rainfall, growth, harvest, food, birth, life. The night, when a*ll the beasts of the forest creep forth,* and the morning, *when they go to lie down in their dens* – while ordinary people have to get up and go to work! (104:20-23)

Throughout, the psalm is addressed directly to God: the creature calls the Creator, "You".

The elephant in the tree: the hyrax. (Photo: D. Connolly)

> *You send forth your spirit, and they are created,*
> *and you renew the face of the earth.* (104:30)

It is only at the very end that the singer steps outside the song, as if to review and confirm it, and to address us: *I will sing to the Lord all my life, / sing psalms to my God while I live* (104:31-34). And then, the singer finds sin in the world, and would wish it away:

> *Let sinners vanish from the earth,*
> *and let the wicked exist no more.* (104:35)

What kind of sin? I think, in the context, it is sin against creation, against God's handiwork. Our planet existed for billions of years without us humans, and in that time many things have happened to it, both harsh and gentle. But we are a danger to it now. We can do harm to the world: the ground can be cursed and the air poisoned by our greed and foolishness. The Hyrax and the Ibex – and the elephants and the trees – and countless other forms of life, can be lost. We can be lost. Creation comes with a price: we need to care for our world as we might care for ourselves. Otherwise, why sing praise to God?

> *Bless the Lord, O my soul.* (104:35)

(September/October 2011)

Three psalms combine to give a broad picture of Israel's history and how differently it can be assessed. We too might have varying views of our own past.

The Backward Look

Let those who are wise give heed to these things,
and consider the steadfast love of the Lord.
(Psalm 107:43 NRSV)

Once I saw three pictures in an Irish newspaper: a ballet dancer, a footballer who had just scored a goal and a participant at a charismatic prayer meeting. All three were similarly poised with arms raised in grace and glory. Joy, and a common humanity! The pictures were in fact scattered through the newspaper, but set them side by side and they would speak together.

Much the same has happened in the Book of Psalms: for example, at some stage, an inspired editor parcelled three psalms together – three long, stately tellings of the way of God with the people of Israel. They speak the same truth, but from different points of view. In one, a grateful people left their captivity in Egypt "with shouts of rejoicing" (Psalm 105). In another, the Israelites had to be dragged screaming and kicking to the Promised Land: "they scorned the land of promise; they had no faith in his word" (Psalm 106). The third hindsight looks for patterns rather than a story: how does God work with travellers and prisoners, sick people and sailors – what are the wonders God does for the people? (Psalm 107). Each psalm, each backward look, tells a true story, but not the whole truth. Only, let them speak together.

We do as much ourselves in our own backward looking; the histories of our own nations can be very simplified

44

and selective. We can look back over our lives, the times that were in it when we were children and when we were growing up: what kind of a world was it, good or bad, dark or peaceful? And the drums may beat differently for each of us. One memory recalls the settled, secure nature of those days. Another memory is of a more sour, repressive and narrow-minded time. Still another account describes terrible and hidden deeds; attitudes in our society and Church which we took for granted but which did not favour children or freedoms or openness. The past is indeed "a foreign country", and we bring back different souvenirs of our visits there.

All of this is well known; we are forever revisiting our history. But here is what haunts me: what if we were the object of the backward look? Thirty, forty years from now, when they look back at our times what will they be saying? To put it another way, what is going on now, in our own days, that we should be aware of, and not doing – or doing? The order of priorities that once placed slavery and child abuse (it wasn't even called that in those days) and women's rights low on the scale of things: what corresponds today? Could we more thoroughly and generously examine our values now, rather than waiting for the next generation to do it for us?

Different Drummers, the batiks come from Togo, West Africa.

Perhaps what I am looking for is prophecy: not a looking to the future, but an insight into the meaning of our own times and the things we do in them, and the attitudes we hold among ourselves. A prophetic insight, with the conscience to recognise it and the courage to follow it. It is a thing the Church ought to be good at, even if we have often failed in the past. Only, let us speak together.

(May 2005)

Even a longing for freedom and justice can warp into a desire for vengeance – in the time of the psalmist or in our own days.

the snake-charmer's voice

**They are heedless as the adder that turns a deaf ear
lest it should catch the snake-charmer's voice**
(Psalm 58:5-6)

Some psalms can bite. Psalm 58 may well be the most vicious of them all – it is, after all, one of the "cursing" psalms, banned from the breviary. We should approach it with caution. In fact we might begin somewhere else altogether, with Psalm 82:

> *God stands in the divine assembly.*
> *In the midst of the gods he gives judgement.*
> *'How long will you judge unjustly*
> *and favour the cause of the wicked?'*
> (Psalm 82:1-2)

The setting is a heavenly court presided over by God, with ranks of lesser beings – small gods, angels, ministers, magistrates – to whom God entrusts the good governance of the world. And, as Psalm 82 suggests, God is not impressed with the way the world is being run (see Isaiah 3:13-15).

In reality, it is human beings who govern, but sometimes rulers foster the notion that it is at the behest of God that they do so – God's gift to their people. Like the old concept of the "divine right" of kings. Or the assumption that some people, or classes, or castes, or families are born to rule; the others are subjects.

Psalm 58 operates out of the same image of things, but from the underside – from the perspective of the ruled, and overruled. It is deeply resentful of corrupt rulers who claim to "hold divine power": *in your hearts you devise injustices; / your hands deal out violence to the land* (Psalm 58:3). Some rulers wish to start a dynasty: their children are groomed to inherit control. Spoiled rotten! *In their wickedness they have gone astray from their birth: / they wandered among lies as soon as they were born* (Psalm 58:4).

> *Let them vanish like water that runs away:*
> *let them wither like grass that is trodden underfoot;*
> *let them be like the snail that dissolves into slime.*
> (Psalm 58:8-9)

When the oppressed find their voice it may be charged with a deep anger – both at the injustices done to them, and at having for so long accepted the situation. We let them get away with it! It can lead to revenge and a reign of terror: *The just shall rejoice at the sight of vengeance; they shall bathe their feet in the blood of the wicked* (Psalm 58:11). The psalm ends:
"Truly", all shall say, "the just are rewarded.
Truly there is a God who does justice on the earth."
Truly a dubious conclusion!

We're dealing with snakes here, according to Psalm 58: *Their venom is like the venom of the snake* (Psalm 58:5). Snakes are feared as treacherous and deadly; the psalm calls for God to break their teeth, tear out their fangs (Psalm 58:7). But God is a snake-charmer, who does not wish to destroy, but to rid the snake of its venom. No easy task, and not something a snake really wants to hear; but it is a better outcome than vengeance, all the same.

Ink drawing from Nigeria.

(January/February 2012)

Barrowman has Right of Way

If the Lord does not build the house,
in vain do its builders labour;
if the Lord does not watch over the city,
in vain do the watchers keep vigil.

In vain is your earlier rising,
your going later to rest,
you who toil for the bread you eat:
when God pours gifts on the beloved while they slumber.
(Psalm 127)

A bumper-sticker that never was, as far as I am aware: BARROWMAN HAS RIGHT OF WAY.

Brutal work: pushing a handcart or wheelbarrow, laden with cement or planks or trash or water containers, through mud, dirt tracks, ploughed fields, uphill and downhill, between cars and trucks and pedestrians. If, that is, you are lucky enough to have been hired; otherwise it's home hungry at the end of the day. I think it should be standard courtesy for drivers, part of the Highway Code, written into law, that barrowmen are given precedence at all times. They surely earn their crust.

As I see it, the barrowmen stand for all those bonded to drudgery, for those – men, women, children – who do dirty menial work, for long hours, for small reward, with little dignity and no glamour. Some might be maids or minders; some pick over the dumps to gather scrap and other people's throwaways. Many you will not see at all: they are hidden away in sweatshops or slave mines, in slums and shantytowns. They get no respect, and if they are illegal they get no protection.

Years ago an old philosophy teacher told us, "We take God's love for granted, forgetting that it is granted." I think we are also in danger of taking poverty for granted: "You always have the poor with you" (John 12:8). Now, why should that be? Jesus also said, and he was the only one who could say such a thing: "Blessed are you who are poor, for yours is the kingdom of God" (Luke 6:20).

That was defiant. True to form, Jesus was changing the rules, at least the rules we play by. Psalm 127 has the right of it: no matter what you build or own or claim, what is greatest is granted – love and life and joy and children and the very world we live in – all granted, all given to us. *God pours gifts on the beloved while they slumber.*

It ill becomes me, and others like me, to talk of the poor and those who toil for the bread they eat – I who have never in my life wanted for a bite to eat or a place to rest. I cannot cure the poverty and injustice of the world, but I

"Truly children are a gift from the Lord" (Psalm 127). The batik comes from Nigeria, West Africa.

could follow the example of my Lord, who washed the feet of his disciples, touched the untouchable, ate with the outcast, and paid attention to people. Courtesy is not the least of virtues: I could at least give precedence to the barrowmen. In the kingdom of God, it is they and the poor who have the right of way. Maybe I should print and distribute that bumper-sticker!

(January/February 2005)

I use the ICEL English version (1993) of Psalm 113 because of the way it describes God bending down to us. St Paul says much the same in Philippians 2:6-11. Think of the humility of God.

Making a Name

Servants of God, praise,
praise the name of the Lord.
Bless the Lord's name
now and always.
Praise the Lord's name
here and in every place,
from east to west.
(Psalm 113:1-3. ICEL Version 1993)

There are names we are given, and names we make for ourselves. Belfast-woman Jocelyn Bell made a name for herself in astronomy – in 1967, while still a student, she identified the first known pulsar ("a rapidly spinning neutron star that emits beams of radio waves", since you ask). Teresa of Calcutta made a name for herself in works of mercy, as Wangari Maathai made a name for herself by having millions of trees planted across Kenya.

The first lines of Psalm 113 weave a canon of three calls to praise the name of the Lord, always, everywhere. The psalm is the first of a group of psalms, 113 – 118, known as the Great or Egyptian Hallel which was sung especially at the feast of Passover. The Hallel ("Praise") relates especially to the Exodus from Egypt, during which the Israelites learned of the secret, sacred, unutterable Name of God – "I Am Who I Am" (Exodus 3:1-15).

"Gods make their own importance," as Homer's ghost whispered to fellow-poet Patrick Kavanagh; they also make names for themselves by their behaviour. This is what interests the author of Psalm 113, the behaviour of the God of Israel – what kind of name would that make? *"The Lord towers above nations"* (v 4) and *"The Lord bends down..."* (v 6).

"Who compares to our God?" (v 5). Nobody, the psalmist replies; God is beyond comparison. The poet Robert Browning wrote, "God's in his heaven, all's right with the world". But for Psalm 113 God is beyond both earth and heaven: *"The Lord towers above nations, / God's glory shines over the heavens"* (v 4). Our Irish poet Patrick Pearse warned us not to bargain or huckster with God; we sense, but cannot imagine, the mystery behind the Name of God.

Pen-
and-ink
drawing
by
Nigerian
artist
Lowo.

And yet, Psalm 113 says the Lord bends down in a movement of compassion towards two particular classes of people: the scavengers and rag-pickers who live off rubbish dumps (vv 7-8), and the childless, the barren, the parents of dead children (v 9). This, perhaps, we can imagine: God squatting down by the hurt and the heart-broken, as someone might with a lost child, bending at the knees, not just bowing from the waist. Different level, another vision.

I think there is a woman's voice in Psalm 113: *"The childless, no longer alone / rejoice now in many children"* (v 9) (for a male voice, see Psalm 127). The childless Hannah sings for the birth of her son Samuel, and cheerfully inflates the numbers – "The barren has borne seven!" (I Samuel 2:1-10). Centuries later, Mary of Nazareth will magnify the Lord for the unlikely birth of her own son, and for the wonders of a God who "has brought down the powerful from their thrones, / and lifted up the lowly" (Luke 1:46-55).

It was Mary's son who squatted by the hurt and the heart-broken; he became a slave and died like a criminal. "Therefore God highly exalted him and gave him the name that is above every name" (Philippians 2:6-11). It was a name he had already made for himself.

(June 2010)

De profundis

My soul waits for the LORD
more than those who watch for the morning,
more than those who watch for the morning.
(Psalm 130:6 NRSV)

A friend of mine reprimanded me once when I dourly quoted Thomas Kempis: *A joyful night begets a sorrowful morning.* "No! No!" came the reply, "The Psalmist says, *Weeping may linger for the night, but joy comes with the morning"* (Psalm 30:5 NRSV). Another friend, a classmate who had spent fourteen years in the Irish Army before he joined St Patrick's missionaries, spoke of the bleakness of night-time sentry duty, the slumping of his spirit in the small hours, and his longing for the light of day.

The author of Psalm 130, the *De profundis*, (*Out of the depths I cry to you, O LORD!*), may have been an old soldier himself: twice he names the anxiety of the night guard. He knew what he was talking about, as a mother would who was night-watching a sick child.

In the *De profundis*, it was a night-time of guilt and sin; in Psalm 30, sickness and loss; in Psalm 59, voracious enemies (vv 14-16). And for the people of Israel in the time of Isaiah, it was a dark night of war – not all the prophet's words were a comfort to them:
"*Sentinel, what of the night? "*
Sentinel, what of the night?"
The sentinel says:
"*Morning comes, and also the night.*
If you will inquire, inquire;
Come back again."
(Isaiah 21:11-12)
Not even the sentry knows when this night will end.

We are not a species that feels at home in the dark. In northern countries, by November each year darkness is steadily flooding the days; the hours of night increase, and in high latitudes people can suffer from Seasonal Affective Disorder, with its apt acronym SAD. It is a condition of ill-health, depression and lethargy, simply because people are not getting enough sunlight. "The light of day" is not just a figure of speech; it is a biological necessity.

In some countries the night lasts for months; the night-time of the soul can also last for months, or years. And it is not just an individual affliction; it can infect a

nation, or a people, or a church. As with many of the psalms, Psalm 130 turns in the end from the individual to the community, to Israel, to the Church:
O Israel, hope in the LORD!
For with the LORD there is steadfast love,
and with him is great power to redeem.
(Psalm 130:7)

We need to acknowledge the dark night within our Church that is being uncovered in recent years; that when we call on God it truly is out of the depths. And, as the **De profundis** implies, there is great need to repent and make amends:
If you, O LORD, should mark iniquities,
Lord, who could stand?
(v 3)
Yet I believe that, even now, there is hope for us and for our Church, if we watch for the morning, and prepare for what redemption will ask of us as it dawns.

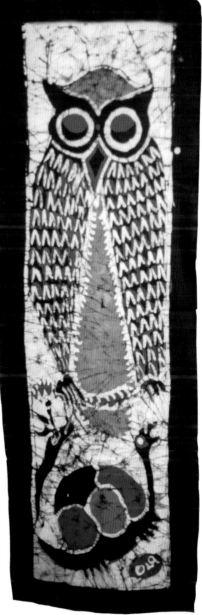

At home in the dark: Owl batik from Nigeria.

(November 2009)

It is likely that most psalms were written by men – that's the way things were, and often still are. But Psalm 131 surely came from a woman's heart and body.

A God of Small Things

O Lord, my heart is not lifted up,
my eyes are not raised too high;
I do not occupy myself with things
too great and too marvellous for me.
But I have calmed and quieted my soul,
like a child quieted at its mother's breast;
like a child that is quieted is my soul.

O Israel, hope in the Lord
from this time forth and for evermore.
(Psalm 131 RSV)

There aren't many prams in Africa; infants are carried on the back or on the hip. I watch this woman from Togo as she pounds cooked yam in a mortar, her free arm curling behind her to steady the baby tied sleeping on her back. It is also a normal and a public thing in Africa that mothers breast-feed their babies. Feeding or sleeping, there is contact, a body-to-body closeness between mother and child – her body knows where and how the child is. As one woman put it, when the time comes her body's aches remind her there is a child to be fed.

But what would I know about any of that, being a man? It is only a woman who had conceived, carried and given birth to a child, who could feel such things in her body and her spirit, and write – as I believe – Psalm 131: it is a woman's experience and insight. The image is of a nursing mother, and the image is of God:
Can a woman forget her nursing child,
or show no compassion for the child of her womb?
Even these may forget, yet I will not forget you.
(Isaiah 49)
God as nursing mother: it would take a woman to say what that might mean.

The Bible can embarrass us with its blunt and earthy language; all the vocabulary of lovemaking, pregnancy, labour and birth is used to express the hands-on love of God for us. The good news of Jesus Christ is equally tangible, tactile – both Bethlehem and Calvary were raw and bloody; and we pray not only for forgiveness, but for our daily bread. The Apostle Thomas

This batik from Togo shows a woman doing one of the most common chores – pounding food for her family. Her baby is snugly asleep on her back, safe in the embrace of her mother's everyday rhythm.

was right: unless I can touch it, I won't believe it. Or unless it touches me. Children know this too, and want to handle the figures in the Christmas Crib.

But at Christmas the image in Psalm 131 changes, and the child at its mother's breast is the Son of God. What sort of role-reversal is this, that God should come to us so intimate, so fragile, so needy? A God of small things – as small as the one-celled beginning of a human life. Maybe I am occupying myself with things too great and too marvellous for me, but I can't help thinking that in Mary's child God is woven into the whole fabric of Creation. Incarnation gets as close in as that. With Christ, God is at home in his skin.

(December 2002)

Psalm 10, an incident from the life of Jesus in Mark 10:32-45, and inter-ethnic violence in an African country mingle to teach a lesson on service of others.

Bad News

They were on the road, going up to Jerusalem;
Jesus was walking on ahead of them; they were
in a daze, and those who followed were apprehensive.
Once more taking the Twelve aside he began to tell them
what was going to happen to him....
(Mark 10:32-45)

A dark mood: the news from Kenya is bad, and the killings continue in Darfur, and from other parts of the world the same grim stories go on and on.
LORD, why do you stand afar off
and hide yourself in times of distress?
The poor are devoured by the pride of the wicked;
they are caught in the schemes that others have made.
(Psalm 10:1-2)
A text message from a friend in Kenya last night: "The murder, rape, burning is outside reason." It is madness, but a madness encouraged to an evil end. *They sit in ambush in the villages; in hiding places they murder the innocent* (Psalm 10:9 NRSV).

For Jesus on the road to Jerusalem in St Mark's Gospel there was a similar grim mood: he strode ahead, alone with his thoughts and his dread; his followers straggled behind him, uneasy and afraid. Three times he warned the Twelve about what was going to happen to him. It is the inevitability of the thing that is so terrifying; nothing can turn this aside: he will die, and it will be a bad death. (Mark 10:32-34)

But the apostles were crass, more concerned about themselves, their seniority, and their prestige. James and John had tried to steal a march on the others, and they resented it. (Mark 10:35-41) Jesus had to take them aside again: *"You know that among the gentiles those they call their rulers lord it over them, and their great men make their authority felt. Among you this is not to happen. No; anyone who wants to become great among you must be your servant, and anyone who wants to be first among you must be slave to all."* (Mark 10:42-44)

These are not guidelines for their spiritual lives, nor are they only for followers of Jesus; they have to do with power and responsibility. When

Times of distress. Batik from Nigeria.

people of power put their own interests first, catastrophe is inevitable - whether it is economic power or political power or military power or religious power. Service of others is not a counsel of perfection; the welfare of the world depends on it.

As always, the poor and the weak pay the greatest price, caught in the schemes of others who have tampered with them, manipulated them, and stolen from them:

> They seize the poor and drag them away.
> They crouch, preparing to spring,
> and the helpless fall beneath such strength.
> (Psalm 10:9-10)

It is at this point that hope comes: *"For the Son of man himself came not to be served but to serve, and to give his life as a ransom for many"* (Mark 10:45). Can death bring life? Can bad news become good news?

(May 2008)

A response to the events of September 11th, 2001.

Echoes of Terror

Let the praise of God be on their lips
and a two-edged sword in their hand,
to deal out vengeance to the nations
and punishment on all the peoples;
to bind their kings in chains
and their nobles in fetters of iron;
to carry out the sentence pre-ordained:
this honour is for all his faithful.
(Psalm 149)

By the time you are reading this it could be six months after the terrorist attacks on New York and Washington – they will still be clearing the rubble from Manhattan, not to mention the Ground Zero in people's hearts. The echoes of terror sound for a long while. What I have to say may no longer be relevant; these closing lines from Psalm 149, from two-and-a-half thousand years ago, will be. But not, perhaps, to our comfort.

What made the act of terrorism so horrifying, to me at least, was not only the wantonness and the magnitude of its cruelty, but that the people doing it, and their supporters, did not seem to see it as wrong or evil. To them, it was noble and justified, worthy of celebration.

Cambodia, Rwanda, the Holocaust, slavery, religious persecution, the oppression of women – the human story is littered with cruelties. And all carried out by people who believed they were in the right: it was pay back time, or they were protecting their values and beliefs, or it was for the good of humanity, or – most awful – it was the will of God.

Certitude is a dangerous thing; it can crowd out compassion and understanding. It can become a heartless conviction that I am right, and the others are wrong and wicked and should not be tolerated. I quote from the seventeenth century Oliver Cromwell: "I beseech you, in the bowels of Christ, think it possible you may be mistaken." Cromwell should have listened to his own words; it might have put some restraint on the things that were done.

Psalm 149 begins as a song of praise, a dance to a delighted God; and suddenly trips over to a vengeful intolerance, and a desire to punish. I don't

"Vengeance is mine, I will repay," said the Lord (Romans 12:19), but all too often in history people have taken over this role with terrible consequences. A marker over one of the mass graves in Cyanika, Rwanda, to the countless thousands slaughtered in and around the church during the genocide of 1994.
(Photo: G Howley)

think this is hypocrisy; it just reflects the way we are. I find light and shadow co-existing in myself, as they do in the psalm. And I can be blind to both the light and the darkness. I suppose it's the need for redemption in me.

Do you think it couldn't happen to you, or to any of us? It happened in the Psalms, which had their origins in Judaism, and are today prayed by both Jews and Christians. Do we mean what we say when we use these words from Psalm 149? There were times in our history when we did.

(March 2002)

Joyful Noise

O come, let us sing to the Lord;
let us make a joyful noise
to the rock of our salvation!
(Psalm 95 NRSV)

Although it happened many years ago, I have a strong memory from the burial of Bishop Thomas McGettrick in St. Theresa's Cathedral at Abakaliki, Nigeria, in January 1989: the organ was playing while the choir was chanting *In Paradisum deducant te angeli* while an army chaplain in the sanctuary blared the Last Post on a bugle while a local musician was sounding a cow's horn in traditional mourning while a civil defence group blew shrill whistles while altar servers clinked thuribles in their chains while outside there was a series of thunderous cannon blasts – all at the same time as the body was being carried from before the altar to the crypt where it was to be laid. A general clatter in praise of God and in tribute to a good man. Joyful noise, indeed!

There are ancient echoes here:
Sing praise with sound of trumpet,
Sing praise with lute and harp…
Sing praise with resounding cymbals,
Sing praise with clashing of cymbals. (Psalm 150)
Not all worship in Africa – or in the psalms – would be as exuberant as that, but you'd want to allow for it. Praise can be as explosive as a head of steam, and as unstoppable.

When we wish to praise, we clap hands: we beat our palms together and make a noise – amazing, when you think about it! But it's what we do: we make noise, we shout and holler, we bang things, we jump to our feet and dance:
"Let them praise God's name with dancing
and make music with timbrel and harp." (Psalm 149:3)
It is how we acknowledge what is good and praise-worthy, even if, in more ordered circumstances, we would also use words and speak coherently.

"Praise the Lord!" is a common cry with preachers and charismatic leaders, but I suspect it sometimes has less to do with actual praise than with crowd control. And, of course, praise can be mercenary, with an agenda. True praise is generous: when you recognise goodness outside and beyond yourself, and are glad of it.

"Making a joyful noise!" The batik comes from Burkina Faso, West Africa.

The Hebrew psalms were called *Tehillim*, "songs of praise"; they reflect the wide range of human experience, and they are generous. To give praise when things go well is good, but it is a small thing: any football fan or race-goer would do as much. It is a different matter to give praise in a time of darkness and despair. When I ask people here in Nigeria how things are with them, and they reply "We thank God for everything", I know something terrible has happened. It is not just resignation on their part, but a faith – and a praise – that is close to defiance.

> *"You are my praise in the great assembly.*
> *My vows I will pay before those who fear God.*
> *The poor shall eat and shall have their fill.*
> *Those who seek the Lord shall praise the Lord.*
> *May their hearts live for ever and ever!"*
> (Psalm 22:27-28)

That from a psalm that begins, *"My God, my God, why have you forsaken me?" (Psalm 22:1)*

(May 2006)

3: Lent/Easter

The Green Blade Riseth

A reflection on the dark days of Good Friday and Holy Saturday, including a parable of a vineyard. (Matthew 21:33-46)

Passion Fruit

O King of the Friday
Whose limbs were stretched on the cross,
O Lord who did suffer
The bruises, the wounds, the loss,
We stretch ourselves
Beneath the shield of thy might,
Some fruit from the tree of thy passion
Fall on us this night!
(Old Irish prayer)

Even so terrible a day as Good Friday has its own poetry. There is a long tradition in which the Tree of the Garden of Eden and the Tree of Calvary echo each other: they are known for the fruit they bore, the one to our destruction, the other to our life and hope. An Irish imagination once fastened on that old insight to give us this prayer of the Cross of Christ and the fruit it carried. But even in poetry fruit is not so simple as it might seem.

For most of us fruit is food, destined for the market and the table, cultivated for colour, shape and shelf life. Fruit is favoured for diet and health – it supplies fibre, energy, vitamins, antioxidants and I don't know what else. Fruit is good for you, and it is displayed in neat rows in the supermarkets, burnished and tamed.

Nature, however, is not really interested in food, certainly not our food. As the plant sees it, fruit is a strategy for survival; it is one of the ways in which plants live on and spread, how they manage time and space. The aim is to entice animals or birds to eat the fruit, so that later – and elsewhere – they might excrete the indigestible seed to fall perhaps on fertile ground. Or, in a different tactic, the flesh of a fruit fallen from the tree could itself be a packed lunch for the seed should it begin to germinate. For nature, fruit is an adventure.

Might it have been the same gamble with the fruit of Calvary's tree – a long shot, a last throw, the vineyard owner sending his own son because the tenants had repulsed his earlier messengers? (Matthew 21). "They will respect my son" – but they didn't, *we* didn't, and so he came to Calvary and his cross. An adventure indeed, with this difference, that while nature is profligate and produces fruit in vast abundance in the hope that at least some will come to growth, God has only the one son. Everything lives or dies by him. It wasn't only the widow who gave all she had to live on; so did God (Luke 21:1-4). For that matter, so did Jesus. Perhaps more than anything else, that is the measure of God's love for us.

This Kenyan "still life" batik cannot hope to capture the wonder of how fruit is a strategy for survival. Fruit is also used as a metaphor to help us comprehend the mystery of Christ's death and resurrection.

Good Friday and the day following are bleak, empty days, and I am often anxious in them to rush on to the Resurrection that I know is the outcome. And, yet, I think it might be better for me to stay with "the bruises, the wounds, the loss" – that's what it felt like at the time, and God knows that's what it has felt like many a time since. Even darkness and loss have their own odd grace: would I not be better waiting with the fruit, lest it awaken to life and no-one there to mark it?

(April 2003)

This is the voice of Mary of Bethany: in the batik from Togo, she is the one on the right, Lazarus her brother is at the centre with the children running to him, and Martha is striding away to the left. All in my imagination, of course.

Ela's Tears

When Mary came where Jesus was and saw him, she knelt at his feet and said to him, Lord, if you had been here, my brother would not have died. When Jesus saw her weeping, and the Jews who came with her also weeping, he was greatly disturbed in spirit and deeply moved. He said, Where have you laid him? They said to him, Lord, come and see. Jesus began to weep.
(John 11:32-35. Read John 11:1-44)

"Lazarus was the favourite. For a while I thought I was the one closest to Jesus, sitting at his feet, hanging on his every word. I know it annoyed Martha, poor dear; she was always so responsible! But it was Ela, as we called him at home, the special one, who never said a thing. Even as children, we knew he needed looking after. He had no sense for schooling; his gift was to draw decency out of people. When he grew older, and had lost his child's attractiveness, people still liked him, and when they were with him felt more like what they could be. And children – they climbed all over him! He overturned tables and scattered the goats at Bethany often enough, but it was from awkwardness, not malice. And he was the master's favourite, though he never asked a question, and half the time fell asleep leaning against him.

"I'm not sure Ela ever realised what had happened to him the day he died, nor four days later when Jesus called him back to the living. And I know he never understood what was done to Jesus in the end – but then, who has ever made complete sense of that?

"Later, I got married and had my own children. Martha never married: she continued to look after Lazarus till he died, for good this time. Of course, it was for good the first time too, though we didn't see it that way then, Martha and I. We really let the Master know how we felt with our pathetic 'Where were you when we needed you?' In the end, he took our breath away when he gave the breath back to my brother: how Ela glowed with delight when he saw Jesus there, and wondered why he was crying like a child. Then he, too, burst into tears of sympathy: when they got the cloths off him, and they held each other, it was hard to tell who was comforting whom.

A batik from Togo, West Africa. Can you imagine that it shows Martha, Lazarus and Mary from the village of Bethany?

"I have sometimes wondered at Jesus' own upset – he was savage with sorrow that day, as if he were angry at something. Maybe it was at himself, that he had not come more quickly. Or was it a greater anguish, at so much suffering, everywhere – all the pain that is part of God's creation? Or what burden was on him, and his own death only days away? You know, I can't think of him dead, and don't know what to make of him risen. What I remember most clearly is the day I anointed him at our home in Bethany – he was so beautiful, but there was the smell of death off him all the same. I wonder did Ela sense it too, in his own way, and that was why he cried?"

*The batik from West Africa helps me to imagine the voice and the scene. But Mary of Bethany did anoint Jesus before his death, "and the house was filled with the fragrance of the perfume" (John 12:1-8, Gospel reading for Monday of Holy Week). This is not mere cosmetics, but change for the Cosmos. (And see **Haircare**, page 100.)*

(April 2004)

A reflection on the forty days of Lent and our journey to Easter.

Road Movie

They are happy, whose strength is in you,
in whose hearts are the roads to Zion.
As they go through the Bitter Valley
they make it a place of springs,
the autumn rain covers it with blessings.
They walk with ever growing strength,
they will see the God of gods in Zion.
(Psalm 84)

There are some movies which are fashioned around a journey – a pilgrimage or a quest, in search or in flight. It might be undertaken walking, or by boat, by horseback and covered wagons, or by motorised lawnmower! The story unfolds in the course of a journey – the journey *is* the story: a journey inwards as much as across a given terrain. They are sometimes called road movies: *La Strada, How the West was Won, Into the West* (a different 'West', in another country!), *The Lord of the Rings, Odyssey*, and its modern equivalent, *2001: A Space Odyssey.*

And there have been several screen versions of The Ten Commandments: the Exodus of the Chosen People from Egypt, and their forty years of wandering in the Sinai desert before they could enter the land that was promised to them. Jesus followed this tradition in his forty days of fasting in the Judean wilderness (Matthew 4). As does Lent and its forty days.

There is not much to Lent these times, or so it seems: two Fast Days, Ash Wednesday and Good Friday, and nothing much above the ordinary in the way of abstinence. If I give up the cigarettes or the drink for the duration, it is probably a private matter. But when I look to the liturgy, it seems to me that Lent is a road movie.

The Sunday Gospels for Lent in Year A (as in this 2005, and every third year after that) were chosen to mark the stages of a journey the catechumens make to their baptism at Easter. Jesus is their companion on the road, and with him they meet some challenging people – the devil in the desert (1st Sunday); Moses and Elijah on the mountain (2nd Sunday); a woman by a well in Samaria (3rd Sunday); a blind man in Jerusalem (4th Sunday); and "a man named Lazarus who lived in the village of Bethany with his two sisters, Mary and Martha" (5th Sunday). The way leads through temptation and transfiguration, unbelief and belief, darkness and light, death and life:

66

Fruit sellers walking to market in a batik from Togo, West Africa.

contrasts that mark any human story. Bitterness and blessings, as Psalm 84 has it. The final stretch of the journey is the toughest, uphill all the way – it too is a journey inwards (Passion Sunday).

I was baptized as an infant; it was many years later that I began to realise what had been done to me. In a sense, that might be a life's work: owning the fact that I was born at all, and owning the rebirth of my baptism. These events belong to my unremembered past but they make me what I am. They are worth exploring, and celebrating – which we do for birthdays but not so much for baptism days. So perhaps it is appropriate that I enter this road movie, and walk the Lenten way with Christ and the catechumens. Who knows what I might learn from the Gospels on the way?

(March 2005)

67

The grief of parents and the grief of God.

"I don't care what he did in Lagos"

**The king was deeply moved, and went up to the chamber over the gate, and wept; and as he went, he said,
"O my son Absalom, my son, my son Absalom!
Would I had died instead of you,
O Absalom, my son, my son!"**
(2 Samuel 18:33)

In the rattle-bag of my mind there is a phrase, wherever it came from: "I don't care what he did in Lagos, he's still my son!" You could imagine it said by the father – or the mother – of the prodigal son. Or by David of his son Absalom. Or, as it might be, by the Father of Jesus: he too had gone away to "a distant country" and squandered his substance with doubtful companions, till it was all gone and his friends left him. But, unlike in the parable of the prodigal son (Luke 15:11-32), he came to a bloody end in the company of criminals. Lagos or London, Johannesburg or Jerusalem, it doesn't matter: it is every parent's nightmare.

I sometimes wonder how autobiographical were the stories Jesus told. What did home teach him of lost coins and the baking of bread and late-night calls from the neighbours? In the village of Nazareth how were the rich regarded; and were Samaritans despised, lepers kept at arm's length, and widows neglected? As his own sexuality matured, what did he learn of love and friendship and loyalty and gracious self-giving? *"No one has greater love than this, to lay down one's life for one's friends"* (John 15:13). As to the parable of the Prodigal Son, did Jesus recall that as a child he had himself been lost once and joyously found, with a good shaking from his mother to teach him manners (Luke 2:41-51)? Farming, fishing, trading, the raising of buildings, the managing of households, the perils of travel – the stories were all around him before ever he fletched them as arrows to a target. Or was it the other way around? That he told the stories first and then had to live them?

Whatever the case, Jesus is the prodigal son, the great wastrel who flung love about as if there were no end to it, and was roundly condemned for the company he kept – women and men, some of them respectable enough, but in the main, sinners and failures and messers of various sorts. Though we can't talk, since we are the company he kept, and still keeps. His friends were his downfall: he held them too close; he joined the gang. Guilty by association. And he died for it.

"He is still my son." Batik from Togo, West Africa.

St Paul, as you might expect, digs more deeply into the earth of it: *"For our sake (God) made him to be sin who knew no sin, so that in him we might become the righteousness of God"* (2 Corinthians 5:21). That is the what and the why of our Easter celebration: a homecoming marked by music and dancing (Luke 15:25). It seems it is our homecoming as much as it is the prodigal's.

Spare a thought for the Father who would do such a thing for us and our whole sorry world: "I don't care what he did in Lagos; he's still my Son, my Beloved: listen to him!" (See Luke 9:35)

(April 2005)

During the ceremonies on Holy Thursday evening, the priest washes the feet of twelve people from the community in imitation of what Jesus did the night before he died. (John 13:1-20)

The Patterns of Power

Jesus got up from the table, took off his outer robe,
And tied a towel around himself.
Then he poured water into a basin
and began to wash the disciples' feet.
(John 13:1-15)

Long before ever I get to them, the feet I wash on Holy Thursday evening are the cleanest feet in the parish. Those chosen for the ceremony wouldn't dream of coming any other way! We are remembering what Jesus did the night before he died. In teaching his Apostles and closest followers, he had said little about drink or drugs or gambling or sex. About greed, yes: *'You received without payment; give without payment'* (Matthew 10:8-10); *'Sell your possessions, and give alms'* (Luke 12:33). And in fact wealth and property have been a menace for the Church and Church leaders ever since. Though I have never liked that mean remark in John's Gospel about Judas with his sticky fingers in the cash box (John 12:6). John could have let that go: poor old Judas had enough on his charge-sheet already.

However, Jesus seemed to have plenty to say about power, and the pride that goes with it, the desire to control and have precedence over others. *'You know that the rulers of the gentiles lord it over them, and their great ones are tyrants over them. It will not be so among you'* (Matthew 20:25). But the Apostles were slow learners, forever arguing about which of them was the greatest: two-pence looking down on a penny! Until finally, during the Last Supper, Jesus began to wash their feet. He must have been desperate – it was a shocking thing to do: slave work. All this is preserved in the Gospels, no cover-up there! The reluctance of Peter to have his feet washed; the pettiness of the others; their cowardice.

As Jews, they would have been well used to purification rituals: full-body immersion in the water, to emerge dripping and cleansed. It was something you did for yourself at times of great significance and need. But Jesus was speaking of service, something you do for others: *'I have set you an example, that you also should do as I have done to you'* (John 13:15). It isn't so much the foot-washing itself, as that we do things for others: it could be cooking or nursing, or wiping babies' bottoms, or praying or fire-fighting or making peace. There are those who spend – and give – their

ክርስቶስ፥
የደቀ፡መዛሙርቱን፡እግር፡
ሲያጥብ፡

The painting of Jesus washing his disciples' feet comes from Ethiopia.

lives for others *'just as the Son of Man came not to be served but to serve, and to give his life as a ransom for many'* (Matthew 20:28).

It's a pity the washing of feet never became a sacrament, like the laying on of hands, or the breaking of bread, or indeed the water-pouring of Baptism. Think what it could mean at the ordination of a priest or a bishop, with its lessons of service and tenderness, humility and care. It is so easy to fall into the patterns of power. We can be tricked by our titles and our clerical isolation. We don't ask or listen enough. Whether as individuals or as an institution we can abuse the authority given to us – it is both greater and less than we imagine. But, like the Apostles, we are slow learners; we too can be petty and fearful, too protective of our own.

It is good for us that, at least once in the year, we wash feet – we too easily forget that we are servants.

(April 2006)

When Jesus entered Jerusalem it was like something out of prophecy! A humble approach, but a decisive one – it sets the tone for our Holy Week.

Riding to Jerusalem

I bind this day to me for ever,
By power of faith, Christ's incarnation,
His baptism in the Jordan River,
His death on the Cross for my salvation.
His bursting from the spiced tomb,
His riding up the heavenly way,
His coming at the day of doom
I bind unto myself today!
(*St Patrick's Breastplate*)

It was one of my favourite early morning walks during the months I spent in Jerusalem a few years ago: out the Lion's Gate and across to walk along the ridge of the Mount of Olives; then swing down to pick up the road from the desert, past Gethsemane and across the Kidron Valley and back uphill to the walls of the Old City. Coming from the east, the rising sun reddened the city before me. A well-known track for Jesus, or for anyone walking from Bethany or Jericho – until the day he came riding to Jerusalem.

All four Gospels tell of it. That was the intention of course: this was meant to stick in the memory (Mark 11:1-11; Matthew 21:1-11; Luke 19:28-40; John 12:12-19). Reading the accounts you get the impression that Jesus had planned for it. "He'll have a donkey ready; tell him I need it now!" What was he at? Like prophets before him, he was acting out a message. The crowd caught the mood of the thing and joined in, spreading their cloaks and leafy branches on the road before him, and singing from Psalm 118. *"Hosanna! Blessed is the one who comes in the name of the Lord"* (Psalm 118:26 NRSV).

They, and later his chroniclers, well-versed in the Hebrew scriptures, had no difficulty situating the gesture – not only prophecy, but the fulfilment of prophecy:

> *Rejoice greatly, O daughter Zion!*
> *Shout aloud, O daughter Jerusalem!*
> *Lo, your king comes to you:*
> *triumphant and victorious is he,*
> *humble and riding on a donkey,*
> *on a colt, the foal of a donkey.*

(Zechariah 9:9; Matthew 21:4-5)

Jesus was not a proud Captain at the city gates, accepting its surrender; nor indeed the anointed King of Psalm 2, ruling *"with a rod of iron"*. His was the rule of one who had come *"not to be served but to serve, and to give his life as a ransom for many"* (Mark 10:45). Not force nor coercion nor dominance, but service. It was his Way.

It takes the Church eight days to tell this tale. Palm Sunday has our own outburst of acted prophecy when we too carry branches and recall his riding to Jerusalem. Then, through Holy Week, we follow the final days of his life when he is set against every power and ruler and authority

"Man on a Donkey": an indigo batik from Nigeria by Nike Davies-Okundaye.

in the city. He is despised and disfigured and defeated at every step of the way; they win every round until he is dead – and he rises beyond them every time. He will rise, and they will always wonder how it happened.

It is all of a piece: his riding to Jerusalem and his "riding up the heavenly way", as the prayer has it. There was ever only the one journey in his life.

(April 2007)

The Forty Foot

Each year you give us this joyful season
when we prepare to celebrate the paschal mystery
with mind and heart renewed.
(Preface for Lent 1)

The Forty Foot is a well-known swimming place in Dublin in Ireland. Not a beach, not for deck chairs or picnics with small children, but a rugged confrontation of sea and granite. Is it actually forty feet deep? Who knows? How do you measure such things? Whatever the case, forty is a good round number, with toughness and substance. You'd get your depth in it.

Forty is a respected number in the Bible. For the Israelites to wander for forty years in the wilderness was worth remembering. Moses fasted, and Elijah walked, for forty days in the desert, and had spectacular meetings with God at the end. The prophet Jonah brandished the weight of it when he came bawling through the streets of the world's most wicked city, *"Forty days more, and Nineveh shall be overthrown!"* (Jonah 3:4). And in our own times, as you might say, *"(Jesus) fasted forty days and forty nights, and afterwards he was famished"* (Matthew 4:2). Forty is a good round number.

With a pedigree like that, it was inevitable that forty days of fasting would become a practice among Christians. And so it did, at first as a way of remembering Jesus' own fast in the desert after his baptism; but soon it was turned around and, from about the 4th century AD, it began to be a time of preparation for Easter. In a word, Lent.

But why would you need forty days to prepare for Easter? Possibly because it took about fourteen billion years, the age of the universe, to prepare for Easter. As we look back down the billions of years since that beginning, it's as if Jesus lived only seconds ago – and yet we hold that "through him all things were made" (Creed).

This is a stupendous claim our Faith makes, which we dare not diminish; it has been there from Gospel times: *"All things came into being through him, and without him not one thing came into being"* (John 1:3). And the world's future is bound up with the death and resurrection of Christ, as *"through him God was pleased to reconcile to himself all things, whether on earth or in heaven, by making peace through the blood of his cross"* (Colossians 1:20).

What exactly all this means goes beyond us, of course; this is the territory Saint Paul warned us about, where eye has not seen and ear has not heard nor has it entered into human mind to understand (see 1 Corinthians 2:9). Well, what did we expect? It's God's ways we're talking about!

There is a toughness and substance to the forty days of Lent though not as tough as it used to be, as you may remember. Still, like the Forty Foot, you'd get your depth in it. That seems to be the intention: Lent is a time for plumbing the deep places, for searching the mind and heart, for trying to comprehend *"the breadth and length and height and depth, and to know the love of Christ that surpasses knowledge"* (see Ephesians 3:18-19). That's deep enough for anyone.

Batik from Nigeria

(March 2008)

75

We need to take incarnation seriously – Jesus was like us in all things except sin. He had to learn, as we learn: "And Jesus increased in wisdom and in years..." (Luke 2:52).

Called To Training

Then he went down with them and came to Nazareth, and was obedient to them....And Jesus increased in wisdom and in years, and in divine and human favour.
(Luke 2:51-52)

When I was a lad, the top scorers in the nation-wide Leaving Certificate Examination at the end of secondary school in Ireland were invited to become school teachers. Such was the high regard in which teachers were held – they were the pick of the bunch. It was proudly referred to as being "Called to Training", without any need to explain what the training might be for. Could you say that Jesus was called to training? The gospels contain many occasions when, even as an adult, he was taught, influenced, chastened or changed by people that he met.

At a wedding in Cana, when the wine at the meal ran out, his mother urged him to do something: he livened up the party by changing water into wine – and his own life changed with it (John 2:1-11). One of my own first teachers in the Scriptures, an tAth. Tomás Ó Curraoin SPS, wrote of it that Mary was "the eternal woman provoking man (in this case the God-man) to excellence." That excellence would be achieved at the hour of his passion.

Jesus was impressed by an officer in the Roman army of occupation who taught him a lesson in the use of authority: *"For I also am a man under authority, with soldiers under me; and I say to one, 'Go', and he goes, and to another, 'Come', and he comes..."* (Matthew 8:5-13). Another foreigner, a Canaanite woman, rebutted his rudeness to her, and won him over by her wit and her faith. She also challenged the narrowness of his vision: it is not only the *"lost sheep of the house of Israel"* who may eat at the Lord's table (Matthew 15:21-28). He should widen his horizons!

He learned those lessons well: after his resurrection he told his apostles, *"All authority in heaven and earth has been given to me. Go therefore and make disciples of all nations..."* (Matthew 28:18-20).

Perhaps, like many men, Jesus had to learn his own emotions. Arriving too late for the burial of Lazarus, he was lofty with Martha, seeming to offer her only the cold comfort of her brother's resurrection on the last day. But

"Taking the form of a slave": batik from Nigeria.

her sister Mary's desolation broke through his reserve and brought him to tears: *"When Jesus saw her weeping, and the Jews who came with her also weeping, he was greatly disturbed in spirit and deeply moved... Jesus began to weep"* (John 11:17-35). He was the better man for it.

The Word made flesh was truly human, and it seems, like any of us, he had to learn what we Irish call *ciall cheannaithe*, the wisdom we buy through the lessons of life. Being "called to training" belongs to the mystery of the Incarnation; it is even part of the scandal of the cross. For there were other lessons he had to learn, as the Letter to the Hebrews reminds us: *"Although he was a Son, he learned obedience through what he suffered"* (Hebrews 5:7-10). Or as St Paul put it, Christ Jesus *"emptied himself, taking the form of a slave... and became obedient to the point of death – even death on a cross. Therefore God also highly exalted him"* (Philippians 2:6-11). And so he excelled.

(March 2009)

This batik from West Africa speaks to the condition of our Church in these days especially, but it is still alight!

Dark Candle

May the light of Christ, rising in glory,
dispel the darkness of our hearts and minds.
(Prayer at the lighting of the Easter Candle)

The Easter Candle has the creamy yellow colour of common wax candles. There is high drama when it is lit on an Easter night, and all the other candles take fire from it, and the darkness of the death of Christ is driven not only from our hearts and minds, but from the very night itself. Alleluia! But the Easter Candle in this Nigerian batik is dark.

Throughout the rest of the year the Easter Candle stands in our churches, lit only for particular occasions but always there, a witness to the risen Christ: Lumen Christi! And what of the wax-coloured remnants of the candles we ourselves lit on that Easter night, stubs now broken or soiled or used up? We tend to keep a Christening candle, but Easter-night candles get lost. A pity, for we too are witnesses. "You are the light of the world" was not said just to the leaders or to the Apostles, but to the great crowds who followed Jesus *"from Galilee, the Decapolis, Jerusalem, Judea, and from beyond the Jordan"* (Matthew 4:25).

It's not easy being a witness, letting your light shine, practising what you preach; much easier not to preach at all! St Paul had the nerve to say, *"Be imitators of me as I am of Christ"* (I Corinthians 11:1). That, as they say, is a hard act to follow. Yet you cannot speak with authority if your actions do not match your words; in fact, it is the actions that give the best witness. The life lived. We know this; but we also know what we are capable of.

When I look back along the lines of my own life I can see how often I took the low road rather than risk the high, was silent when words were called for or, like Peter, shunned the love of Christ: *"Go away from me, Lord, for I am a sinful man!"* (Luke 5:8). Dark candle.

Power and betrayal are close companions; they test the integrity of political leaders, the police, the military, those who control wealth, doctors, lawyers, bishops, priests; anyone who has dominance over another. It could even be within a family or a household. Betrayal of trust has cast a shadow across the Church from the beginning, has caused dreadful harm, and is heartbreaking in our own times. Dark candle, have you no light that shines?

We have been learning some hard lessons in the past few years, and much has still to be done in the name of justice and compassion and basic civil decency. We may have forgotten how fierce is the justice of God in defence of the weak:

> May he defend the poor of the people
> and save the children of the needy
> and crush the oppressor.
> (Psalm 72)

I find hope in an unlikely image, as shocking in his time as it would be in our own: Jesus eating with a bunch of tax-collectors and sinners, scumbags and social outcasts, abused and abusers (Mark 2:15-17). His was not the death of a hero, not something to inspire us: *"He had no form or majesty that we should look at him, nothing in his appearance that we should desire him"* (Isaiah 53:2). And yet, I believe that Jesus, who died a dark candle in the heart of darkness, teaches us the hardest and most hopeful lesson for our time: God's forgiveness is a gift; you do not have to earn it, but you do have to live up to it.

Batik from Nigeria, West Africa.

(April 2009)

79

Things can happen that challenge our faith in a God of love and mercy. There are no easy answers, and sometimes no comfort at all.

Refusing to be Comforted

A voice is heard in Ramah,
lamentation and bitter weeping.
Rachel is weeping for her children;
she refuses to be comforted for her children
because they are no more.
(Jeremiah 31:15; Matthew 2:18)

It is the feast of the Holy Innocents, three days after Christmas 2009, and I am writing an article to appear in April. It makes for strange connections: Christmas and Easter mingle in my mind. In St Matthew's gospel reading for the day of the Innocents, Joseph is warned in a dream to take *"the child and his mother with you, and escape into Egypt"* (Matthew 2:13-18). Jesus is spared, but there is no warning for the parents of the other boys in Bethlehem; they go down in a horrific slaughter. God does not stop that, any more than he will stop the slaughter of his own son three decades later. How can this be?

Five years ago, almost to the day, a tsunami slashed through the Indian Ocean. It killed over a quarter of a million people. I happened to fly out of Nigeria on the feast of the Holy Innocents that year, 2004, arriving in Ireland to find soul-searching and questioning and discussion, in newspapers, on television and radio, across the whole country. People had responded with magnificent generosity to appeals for help for the devastated countries, but they struggled with the question: How can this be? What kind of God would allow this?

Matthew, writing about the Bethlehem killings, struggled with the same question. He reached back across centuries to the prophet Jeremiah, to a time of devastation and displacement for the people of Israel. The prophet cries that the Lord has saved his people, the remnant of Israel! And he promises in the voice of God, *"I will turn their mourning into joy, / I will comfort them, and give them gladness for sorrow"* (Jeremiah 31), But for some things there is no comfort, and in the middle of Jeremiah's testimony Matthew finds another voice:

> *Rachel is weeping for her children;*
> *she refuses to be comforted for her children*
> *because they are no more.*
> (Matthew 2:18; Jeremiah 31:15)

80

Again in the liturgy for the Innocents, the First Letter of St John reads: *"God is light and in him there is no darkness at all"* (I John 1:5). Yet, there is a darkness that shadows God, at least in our understanding. I think of what can happen to the innocents of our own times. They can die of burns or cancers or other horrors; they can be starved, damaged, abused, lost. They can be deprived of life even before they have had a chance to live it. There is a darkness here, where there should be light. How can this be? What kind of God?

Man and boy: batik from Togo, West Africa.

Holy Saturday is an empty day of mourning for the crucified Christ. This was no play-acting: his death was as real and as terminal as any human death – "dead and buried" as the Creed says. And wouldn't any Father be heartbroken over the loss of his Son? Grief is harsh territory, whether for the parents of a dead child or for God. It was not only the Bethlehem parents, or Rachel, or King David over his son Absalom, but the Father too, who would refuse to be comforted: *"My son, my son, my son, my son! Would God I had died for thee!"* (2 Samuel 18:33). Holy Saturday is as good a day as any to test the mystery of what kind of God.

(April 2010)

81

4: People

Voices in Another Room

I imagine Mary; I recall women I know who might help me understand Mary; I listen to the way the Scriptures speak of her. In a sense, it is all I can do.
(Read John 2:1-11 and Luke 2:41-51)

Imagining Mary

In union with the whole Church
we honour Mary,
the ever-virgin mother of
Jesus Christ our Lord and God.
(Eucharistic Prayer I)

She leaned over him at the table and whispered, "Do you know they're running out of wine?" He gave her a startled look and replied, "Woman, does that concern us? It's not time." Her mind flashed back almost two decades to a 12-year-old in the Temple, so convinced he had a work to do – and now, "It's not time!" To her, it was high time. She squeezed his shoulder affectionately and turned to the anxious waiters: "Just make sure you do whatever he tells you." Then she went back to where the women were.

I'm using my imagination; it's what I have to do for Mary. The Bible tells us very little about her, so we imagine, we use images and poetry: Tower of David, House of Gold, Ark of the Covenant, Morning Star; icons and pictures of Mary as artists and visionaries imaged her at Lourdes, Fatima, Guadalupe.

An uncle of my own did a woodcarving of a Madonna and child: he was an amateur, and her cloak was heavy, but it seemed to me from the first time I saw it that she was walking down a bog road – just as St. John of the Cross imagined:

"With the divinest Word, the Virgin
Made pregnant, down the road
Comes walking, if you'll grant her
A room in your abode."

82

African Virgin and Child. The bible tells us very little about Mary, the Mother of Jesus, so we, like all those of other times, have to imagine what she was like. Is she a real person for us? (Image: Vie De Jésus MAFA, France)

Of course, Mary was also a secondary person in a man's world: I am reminded of some friends of mine, missionary Sisters committed to the rights and dignity of women in a land of much poverty – it is a rich man's world!

Mary knew loss and grief: I remember an aunt in tears scrubbing the floor of the room where her brother had died. Mary reared her child: I think of a mother I know drawing in one of her sons, grown adult, but yet confused at what life can do – "Ah sweetheart! What's wrong?"

I think of the women I know – in my family, among my dear friends. Women who have touched me with their lives, women with compassion in their hands. I believe it is from them that I, a man, can learn what it is to be Woman – as Jesus called his mother at Cana and at Calvary (John 2:4 and 19:26). Mary is a woman who said "Yes!" when she was asked; she kept her word, and God's Word.

(May 2001)

"Show me your friends and I'll tell you who you are." Here are some of Jesus' friends.

A Woman at a Well

Father, hear the prayers of the family you have gathered here before you. In mercy and love unite all your children wherever they may be. *(Eucharistic Prayer III)*

She flinched at his words as if she had been beaten. It was the hottest time of day, the time she usually came to the well for water, and she had found him there ahead of her. Well, she had met worse in her life than a tired man who asked her for a drink, even if he was a Jew. They chatted lightly on what seemed like little matters; he listened carefully to her – she wasn't used to that. It was pleasant, she flirting a little with him – until he told her to call her husband. It surprised her how much that hurt! She slumped against the rim of the well and muttered over her shoulder, "I have no husband." Nor had she, nor much luck with men in general. Jesus stayed, listening. In the end, not all her talk could stop Jesus entering her heart, as St Augustine said, and she believed in him. (John 4)

There are other accidental heroes in the gospels. The one-out-of-10 who took the time to say thanks for being healed of his leprosy – "And he was a Samaritan" (Luke 17). The soldier in the occupying Roman army, who believed Jesus could heal his servant: a man well-used to command, he humbly asked (Matthew 8). The glib Gentile woman in Tyre: she answered the rudeness of Jesus with a smart remark of her own, and got what she wanted from him (Mark 7). And all the other strangers and cast-offs and lowlifes that Jesus mixed with, including a Samaritan woman of doubtful reputation at Jacob's well. He reached across all the barriers of nationality, class, religion, gender and piety; it was as if these things didn't matter to him. So how is it they matter so much to me?

I came across a version of the Good Samaritan parable once in which an Apache carried a wounded white man into a town in the old American West. There was an old hostility between Jews and Samaritans; Jesus was being provocative when he told that story (Luke 10). And yet, such things do happen: in the country where I live, in the heat of religious rioting a few months ago, there were Muslims who rescued and sheltered Christians from mortal danger for two, three, four days until it was safe for them to come out of hiding. Why did I feel so hopeful, and so ashamed, when I heard about that?

Jesus didn't seem to think in terms of us and them. I'm afraid I do: I am much more at ease with us – in my own group, with people who speak my language, who hold the same values that I do. As Eucharistic Prayer 3 puts it in "the family you have gathered here before you", where I know I belong, and who belongs with me. And then the same prayer explodes even that small comfort when it goes on to talk about "all your children wherever they may be." That's a very large constituency! As wide as the world and all its peoples. The woman at the well, the beggar in the doorway, the enemy in ambush, the refugees on the boats, the apocalyptic *"huge number impossible to count"* – are they really all God's children too? All of them my sisters and brothers? Is this what Jesus saw? It would change your life, if you lived by it. It would change the world.

The well was the village gathering place and having to go alone was a sign of the community's displeasure. This batik is from Togo.

(April 2002)

In Acts of Apostles 16:11-40 Paul preaches in Philippi, meets with trouble, and finds an unexpected ally in the person of Lydia, a successful businesswoman.

The Woman Who Sold Colour

A certain woman named Lydia, a worshipper of God, was listening to us; she was from the city of Thyatira and a dealer in purple cloth. The Lord opened her heart to listen eagerly to what was said by Paul. When she and her household were baptised, she urged us, saying, "If you have judged me to be faithful to the Lord, come and stay at my home." And she prevailed upon us.
(Acts 16:14-15)

Lydia was a strong person; you would find her like among the traders and "cash madams" in any market. Bossy, competent, successful, generous, loyal – certainly no fool! What a fine, manipulative invitation she gave to the apostles: "If you have judged me to be faithful to the Lord, come and stay at my home." How could you refuse that? As Luke, the author of Acts of Apostles, and who was there that day, wryly put it, she "prevailed" on them. Lydia was probably good at prevailing.

Her business was at the luxury end of the market: rich clothes, fashionable dress, and especially the very expensive 'Tyrian purple'. It refers to a dye produced from a particular kind of shellfish found near Tyre, in the eastern Mediterranean. 'Royal Purple' – it was said that only kings and the very wealthy could afford it. Lydia's own home place Thyatira, in present-day western Turkey, was famed for its purple cloth; she had obviously brought the trade with her from there to Philippi, in Greece. Not far – only 250 miles or so from her source of supply. And I imagine that, like the Capable Wife in the Book of Proverbs poem, she modelled her own goods:
> *"She makes herself coverings;*
> *her clothing is fine linen and purple."*
> (Proverbs 31:22)
A good ad for the stock she sold. As they say, if you've got it, flaunt it!

Lydia was not a Jew, but a Gentile who worshipped the God of the Jews and who knew their story. When Paul came with the gospel of the crucified Christ – he never preached anything else, a scandal to the Jews and madness to the Gentiles (I Corinthians 1:23) – this hard-headed business woman opened her heart to it. In Luke's other writing, his gospel account, he had an eye for injustice and poverty, and "purple and fine linen" were typical of the uncaring rich (Luke 16:19). Here in Philippi he meets someone who sells purple, and who could count rich and royal among her customers. Yet he noted it didn't stop her offering the apostles a safe house after they'd had trouble with some of the locals (Acts 16:40). She was a foundation member of the Christian community there, and fearless.

The batik from Togo, West Africa, shows a traditional cloth market.

I wonder what Lydia felt when she heard the other story, how the soldiers had woven a crown of thorns and put it on the head of Jesus, and dressed him in a purple robe – wherever they got it! "So Jesus came out, wearing the crown of thorns and the purple robe. Pilate said to them, 'Here is the man!'" (John 19:2-5). He could have been proclaiming the gospel. However old and worn the purple cloth might have been, it still had majesty in it.

(September/October 2004)

Two women who were given fullness of life by Jesus; two stories entangled in the memory of the Church; two voices that spoke to my imagination; two images in a beautiful batik from India.

Straight-up Lady, Living Girl

He fell at Jesus' feet and begged him to come to his house, for he had an only daughter, about twelve years old, who was dying. As he went, the crowds pressed in on him. Now there was a woman who had been suffering from haemorrhages for twelve years…
(Luke 8:40-56; Mark 5:21-43; Matthew 9:18-26)

"I was certain if I could only touch him I would be cured; I did, and I was. He knew it immediately, turned and singled me out of the crowd. There, in front of everyone, the whole story came out, but I didn't care. I had been hiding myself for long enough; powders to cover my smell, the loneliness, the shame. I faced him as I was, triumphant, grateful, happy, whole.

"I would have liked to talk with him, woman to man, but they were dragging at his clothes, rushing him away to another place, some dying girl. I followed them to the house: he was too late, the girl had died, and the mourning music had begun. But he said, no, she was only sleeping, and cleared the crowd from the house. I slipped through their derision (I'd had years of practice at it!) and reached the doorway of the room where she lay. By the time I got there, it was over – the parents were petrified, torn between joy and fear; his three companions were wide-eyed and silent; Jesus was hunched at the bedside, like someone utterly drained. The girl was lying on her side, looking across the width of the room, at the doorway, at me. Our gaze…"

"…met, and we stared at each other. She was a young woman, not tall; I'm tall for my age. Her clothes were drab – I could barely see her in the dim light of the room. But she stood straight up, like a flower unfolded. Her colours seemed to come from inside her, new, washed, fresh. I thought of my sickness, the fever, the tiredness, and the long going away. They say I died: what does that mean for me?

"I felt someone touch me: Jesus had put his hand on mine; he looked at me and asked quietly, 'Are you hungry?' I nodded, yes, and looked back at the doorway. She was gone. I'd like to have spoken with her – for some

reason I think she might be able to explain what has happened to me. I feel like I've been given a gift, and I'm not sure what it is, or what to do with it. I hope we will ..."

"...meet someday. She's only twelve; she must have been born just about the time I got – sick. After what happened to me, the beatings, the force, the betrayal, the agony and then the years of sickness and shame, it's as if I have been given back to myself. All that had been taken from me was worthless to those who took it. He gave me back my life, as he did for the girl. And he saw the worth and the wonder of me – perhaps these she has yet to find."

It has always fascinated me the way the stories of these two women are intertwined across three Gospel tellings, Matthew, Mark and Luke. I don't know if they ever met, but in the memory of the Church they have never been separated.

Two women: batik from India.

It seems from Mark 15:40 that the mother of James and John was called Salome. Here I imagine her voice and her anxiety for the welfare of her two sons.

Sons of Thunder

Then the mother of the sons of Zebedee came to him with her sons, and kneeling before him, she asked a favour of him. And he said to her, "What do you want?" She said to him, "Declare that these two sons of mine will sit, one at your right hand and one at your left, in your kingdom."
(Matthew 20:20-28; See also 4:21-22; 27:55-56)

"He called them the 'Sons of Thunder'. Well, it wasn't from Zebedee they got it; a more placid man I never met. He would have spent his whole life fishing, never saw anything beyond that, for himself or for his sons. So when they walked out on him, it took him between wind and water: he sat there in the boat with his mouth opening and closing like one of his fish. Didn't know what to say. I was happy enough about it at the time; there was no future in Galilee for James and John. Jesus would be good company for them, I felt – he was a nice, sensible boy from Nazareth, a carpenter like his father. There's always work for a carpenter; not like fishing, with its wind and sea and market, and you couldn't trust any of them. Especially my dread: the sea.

"Then – this might seem strange – I decided to go walkabout myself, at my age! Zebedee didn't know what to say this time either, but he'd manage on his own for a while. I wanted to keep an eye on the boys, and I have to say I wasn't happy with what I found. I was surprised at Jesus; all this talk of the meek inheriting the earth, the first coming last, not standing up for yourself: that wasn't the world that I lived in.

"So, one day I hauled the pair of them up and put their case to Jesus. They were embarrassed – you know the jokes they tell about Jewish mothers! And then something astounding happened: Jesus answered, 'You don't know what you are asking. Are you able to drink the cup that I am about to drink?' I knelt there, staring at him in shock – until the boys said, 'We are able' and I realised I had misheard him: he hadn't been talking to me, but to my two lads. And of course, they were game for anything – they were young, they were brash, they were 'Sons of Thunder!'

"But for me it was too late, I had taken the bait: my heart had betrayed me and had already responded, 'Yes, I am able!' I knew what he was talking about – his death in Jerusalem. Till that moment I hadn't taken

Fishermen casting their nets as portrayed in a batik from Nigeria.

him seriously, though I think the other women, Mary Magdalene, Joanna, Susanna and the rest, had realised it already – long before I, or the men, did. The men were still arguing about which of them was the greatest, God help us! And my little foray with James and John hadn't helped.

"What I didn't expect was that the cup would be given me to drink so soon, and that it would be so bitter. Within days he was dead – they got him, as he told us they would. The men mainly ran – that hurt! We few countrywomen watched him die, holding one another when we couldn't hold him. And we never did get to do our woman's thing, to clean up the body and anoint it – the last rites a woman can give. It was all taken out of our hands. But, I have to admit, it was wonderful in the end.

"Well, I came home to Galilee, to my Zebedee – but without my sons. They're gone from me now, but it wasn't the sea that took them, as I'd always feared, but a carpenter who had turned to fishing."

(March 2006)

The first 25 years of St Patrick's (1932-1957 AD) seem to echo the first 25 years of the Church's growth (32-57 AD). Threaded through the article are greetings from St Paul to his friends in Chapter 16 of the Letter to the Romans, written in 56 or 57 AD.

Romans 16

"I commend to you our sister Phoebe, a deacon of the church at Cenchreae...for she has been a benefactor of many and of myself as well." (Romans 16:1-2)

It intrigues me now that I joined a missionary society only twenty-five years after it had been established. In the same early days with the "Founding Fathers", you might say; some of them were still alive in that year, 1956. I knew them! Like being a companion of the Apostles – if not an actual Peter or a Paul, at least a Timothy or a Titus. As you can see, I'm a bit impressionable, easily carried away. Dream on!

Greet Prisca and Aquila, who work with me in Christ Jesus.... Greet also the church in their house.

But it's not a totally fanciful idea; in fact, it is strangely familiar. During the first twenty-five years after Christ, roughly 32 – 57 AD, the Apostles and others had been criss-crossing the Eastern Mediterranean, telling the story, celebrating the memory of Jesus, probing the mystery of the very good news they were proclaiming. And wherever they went, they were founding communities, churches of Christians – not entirely unlike what the missionaries were doing in Nigeria and Kenya during the St Patrick Fathers' own first twenty-five years, 1932-1957.

Greet Andronicus and Junia, my relatives who were in prison with me; they are prominent among the apostles, and they were in Christ before I was.

During those same years, whole networks developed, of friends and family, benefactors and believers, who supported the spreading of the Gospel: but am I now referring to the first century or the twentieth? The patterns are the same, with a similar organic growth. St Paul had written letters to several such communities across present-day Greece and Turkey and Italy, letters that name many of his friends: Stephanas, Philemon, Aquila and Prisca (several times!); *"Greet Rufus...and his mother – a mother to me also"* (See Romans 16 for this and the other quotations; also I Corinthians 16; Philippians 4; Philemon). The records of St Patrick's too contain many

Oil painting titled *Unity* by Nigerian artist Kehinde Babatunde. We sing and celebrate together.

names from the early days: valiant and faithful supporters, our life-blood, our "co-workers, whose names are in the book of life" (Philippians 4:3).

Gaius, who is host to me and to the whole church, greets you. Erastus, the city treasurer, and our brother Quartus greet you.

There is no doubting the affection of St Paul for his friends "whom I love and long for" (Philippians 4:1). But he also refers to "churches" – individual communities of believers which welcomed and supported the spread of the Gospel. In the next fifty years "church" would take on a deeper meaning: "Christ is the head of the church, the body of which he is the Saviour" (Ephesians 5:23); and around 100 AD, Ignatius of Antioch first refers to the "catholic church" – the universal body of believers. But for Paul in 56 or 57 writing to the Romans, the churches he knew were more like our parishes or even small communities. They gave him heart. That's a thing that might be familiar to a missionary, or indeed to any minister of the Gospel anywhere.

Greet one another with a holy kiss. All the churches of Christ greet you.

(March 2007)

93

Nobody comes out completely unsullied from this triangular narrative, least of all Abraham. Genesis chapter 15, to chapter 21:21. But it explains how Abraham is the "Father in Faith" of Jews, Christians and Muslims.

The Other Woman

But Abram said to Sarai, "Your slave-girl is in your power; do to her as you please." Then Sarai dealt harshly with her, and she ran away from her.
(Genesis 16:6)

She was a slave. As is often the case with slavery, when we meet her first it is in someone else's story. That was the story of Abraham and Sarah, and the promise: *"I will make of you a great nation"* (Genesis 12:2). They leave their country to journey to a distant land, though Sarah *"was barren; she had no child"* (Genesis 11:30). Nor would she for twenty-three years: a long time, and for a woman who was already old. But at last a child is born, and a lineage – the familiar cadence of the Jewish and Christian stories: Abraham, Isaac, Jacob…

But there was another story, for there was another woman. After ten years of her own barren waiting, Sarah had taken *"Hagar the Egyptian, her slave-girl, and given her to her husband Abraham as a wife"* (Genesis 16). It was a desperate ploy, and led to a passion of jealousy, bitterness, pride and prejudice between the two women. In the darkness of it, Sarah drove the pregnant Hagar out of the house and into the desert, where she almost died. But she was sent back, and her son was born. *"And Abraham said to God, 'O that Ishmael might live in your sight!'"* (Genesis 17:18).

Thirteen years later the row still rankled. When Sarah finally gave birth to her own child, she could not bear that Ishmael – now almost of age – might *"inherit along with my son Isaac"*. Hagar and her son were sent away again, *"and she departed, and wandered about in the wilderness of Beersheba"* (Genesis 21:20-21). In the end, she wandered out of the Bible entirely – out of Sarah's story and into her own.

Hagar had heard God's word in the wilderness: *"Come, lift up the boy and hold him fast with your hand, for I will make a great nation of him"* (Genesis 16, 21). When she left Abraham's household finally, she took this promise with her along with her son. Egyptian herself, she *"got a wife for him from the land of Egypt"* (Genesis 21). And her story begins to find its fulfilment: Ishmael became the father of "twelve princes", twelve tribes, that lived mainly in the deserts of Arabia (Genesis 25:7-18).

Woman and Child: Pen and ink drawing from Nigeria, West Africa. The woman turns away from us with her child tied to her back. We do not see her face; just one hand that reaches out behind her – in parting? in longing? in loss?

It can happen in the desert that a stream will sink into the sand only to emerge above ground somewhere else. Hagar's story largely fades from the Bible, but surfaces again centuries later, in another scripture, and a different tradition. Arab ancestry was traditionally traced back to Ishmael and his mother Hagar, and so to Abraham, of whom the Qur'an says, "Follow the religion of Abraham, the upright one". In Islamic tradition it is even Ishmael, and not Isaac, that is almost sacrificed by his father. The Hajj, the pilgrimage to Mecca every adult Muslim is expected to make, was inspired by the wanderings of Hagar and Ishmael in the wilderness.

There is an otherness, an estrangement, in Hagar's story; it passed to her son: *"he shall live at odds with all his kin"* (Genesis 16:12). And yet if there is anything these stories tell us, it is that we are, all of us, kin: Jew, Christian, Muslim.

(September/October 2007)

95

I am imagining the voice of Rahab, a prostitute in the city of Jericho. She has to make a terrible choice, and live with its consequences.
Read all of Joshua Chapter 6.

City on Lockdown

Now Jericho was shut up inside and out because of the Israelites; no one came out and no one went in.
(Joshua 6:1)

"The spies from the Israelites thought it best to come directly to my place: no one would take much notice of a couple of men hiding their faces and slipping into the house of Rahab, the prostitute. But Jericho was really a small town, and they were spotted anyway. The city guards were soon pounding on my door, calling on the strangers to come out. But I tricked them, sent them down the road to the river, and sent the two Israelites up the hills to hide. I betrayed my Canaanite people and made my pact with the enemy: my life for theirs, and my family to go free, too.

"Why did I do that? Well, think back: those were frightening times. Everyone knew the Israelites were coming and we were in trouble. We had heard the stories of the Red Sea and the Egyptians and of anyone else who had tried to stop the Israelites. The great days of Jericho were long gone; we were no threat to them. We just happened to be in their way. All we could do was lock down the city and hope for the best. Besides, the God of the Israelites was very strong, and very choosy. So I made my own choice.

"Did I do right? Well, I thought so, at the time. Joshua sent the two spies into the city again to bring us out, all my family, and they took us to their

Oil painting from Nigeria. Untitled.

camp. We saw all that was done. They killed everyone: every man, woman and child and living animal in Jericho. They burned the city to the ground, and then they cursed it. Only I and my family were spared; the spies kept their word, as I had kept mine.

"I live among the Israelites now. My parents are dead, and my family have scattered. They praise me here for what I did, but even so I don't know that I fully fit in. I'm used to that, though; I've lived on the margins before – people of my old profession often do. But it troubles me at times that I am still alive, and all Jericho is gone. It looks like all of us are gone; they say the land was promised to them, so taken from us. I find it hard to celebrate that.

"Would I do it again? Probably."

The voice of Rahab is in my imagination, of course, but this Canaanite woman is mentioned in despatches by some New Testament writers too: she is praised in the Letter to the Hebrews for her faith "because she had received the spies in peace" (11:31), and in the Letter of James for her good works, "when she welcomed the messengers and sent them out by another road" (2:25). The writers were being faithful to the traditional account of the battle of Jericho, as recalled by the victorious invaders in the Book of Joshua, chapters 2 – 6. But the dispossessed may tell a different story. So I found myself wondering what Rahab herself might say about it.

She also comes into the Christmas story: in the genealogy that opens the gospel of Matthew, Rahab is named as the mother of Boaz, who married Ruth – they were the great-grandparents of King David. A distant descendant of David was "Joseph the husband of Mary, of whom Jesus was born, who is called the Messiah" (Matthew 1:1-16).

(January/February 2008)

Again I am using my imagination, perhaps even more than usually! What Pharaoh's daughter did was astounding and dangerous, and how greatly it turned the story that was about to unfold in Egypt.

Pharaoh's Daughter

So the woman took the child and nursed it. When the child grew up, she brought him to Pharaoh's daughter, and she took him as her son. She named him Moses, "because" she said, "I drew him out of the water."
(Exodus 1:8 – 2:10)

"The King's Guards came to question me a few days ago. They were polite and careful: my father Seti may be dead, and a new ruler on the throne, but I still belong to a royal family. They wanted to know about my son Moses. It's no secret he's back in Egypt, wherever he has been all these years. He is still wanted for murder, they said, and is stirring up old troubles among the Hebrews. They asked if I knew anything about him, had he come to see me? But of course he hadn't; he'd know the house would be watched. I just hope he doesn't break my heart again.

"My father was a harsh, fearful man; he had inherited the Hebrews, and they were too much, too many for him. He tried to quell them with slave labour, but they thrived. And then he tried to destroy them. The whole country was recruited for this wiping out: all the people were commanded to kill the boys, but to let the girls live.

"And that's the way it was on the day I went to bathe in the Nile and found him hidden among the reeds and the bulrushes. When I saw him in the little ark, something blossomed within me: I yearned for him, this child. For a long time I had envied those lively Hebrew women, sitting with their babies, all round and milky. Now I could feel in myself the heart of their contentment.

"Things moved quickly after that. Of course, I knew what was going on; I'm not a fool. The girl turning up so bright and helpful, the convenient Hebrew wet nurse; it was a neat, arranged thing. The dispossessed have ways of getting their own back! But he was mine: I'd lost my heart to him the moment I saw him. By law and power I adopted him – what choice did his family have? I'm not proud of it, but I am glad of it. "I'll raise him to the sun!" I cried, and drew him out of the water.

"And that is how it worked out: his mother nursed and weaned him, and brought him to me, safe and sound. He joined my family – or did I join his? We were bound by a conspiracy now, the three of us women – mother, sister, and daughter-of-Pharaoh.

"I couldn't acknowledge him too openly, but people knew. He was protected. Years later, when he chose to return to his family it almost killed me. Yet I was so proud of him, his sense of rightness, his independence. But his Egyptian education didn't endear him to his own people; no matter how he tried to get back into Hebrew ways, he looked like an Egyptian, he walked like an Egyptian.

"A Pharaoh's daughter doesn't have much mind of her own. Life is laid out for her; all she can hope for are petty rebellions. But when I saved a Hebrew boy from death I was defying an absolute ruler, even if he was my own father. I wasn't the only one; in fact, I have never heard that any Egyptian – the midwives, the soldiers, any of the people – carried out that terrible command, 'Kill the boys, spare the girls!' That pleases me greatly. For good or ill, the Hebrews have their chance. I wonder how my Moses will fare with them."

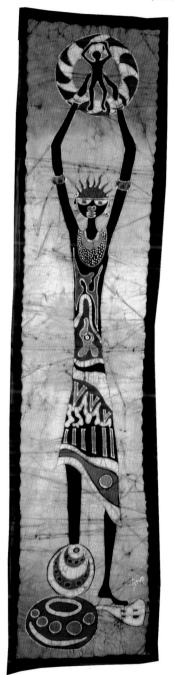

Batik from Nigeria.

(September/October 2008)

I have come across very few comments on the "hair" aspect of these stories; the anointing, yes, but not the loosening of the hair. These accounts are amazing, even shocking, but they have been preserved in the memory of the Church.

Haircare

"As the Lord lives, not one hair of his head shall fall to the ground; for he has worked with God today."
(1 Samuel 14:45)

Among the businesses that I pass each day on my way to the church there is one with a sign that reads, **Legend: Haircare & Property Management.** The synergies in that enterprise would be worth studying!

Jesus on Haircare was encouraging: *"Even the hairs of your head are all counted"* (Matthew 10:30), and *"But not a hair of your head will perish"* (Luke 21:18) – sayings from his own tradition, from the Books of Samuel and of Kings (1 Sam 14:45; 2 Sam 14:11; 1 Kings 1:52). But the haircare given to Jesus himself was of a very different order.

It is a tale twice told in the Gospels. For Luke, a woman *"who was a sinner"* entered a house where Jesus was a guest at a meal: *"She stood behind him at his feet, weeping and began to bathe his feet with her tears and to dry them with her hair"* (Luke 7:36-50). In John's gospel it all took place at Bethany, at the home of Mary, Martha and Lazarus: *"Mary took a pound of costly perfume made of pure nard, anointed Jesus' feet, and wiped them with her hair"* (John 12:1-8).

To Saint Paul, a woman's long hair *"is her glory"* (1 Corinthians 11:15). Or, in the luscious description of the Song of Songs, *"Thy hair is like a flock of goats cascading down from Gilead"* (6:5 Koren). When Judith set out to bedazzle – and behead – the enemy commander Holofernes, she combed out her hair, and *"made herself very beautiful, to entice the eyes of all the men who might see her"* (Judith 10-14). In one of the comic books of my youth, if you'll pardon the example, when quiet Diana Prince takes off her glasses and lets loose her hair she becomes Wonder Woman!

Not to put too fine a gloss on it, it was a sexy thing to do; and on both occasions when it was done to Jesus, it thoroughly shocked all who witnessed it. Except Jesus: he seemed to accept it as his due!

In cultures where women traditionally wear head-ties or scarves, it sometimes happens that they uncover their heads and unbind their hair

Batik from Nigeria.

as a sign of heartfelt grief or protest. I recall an older priest who had spent many years in Africa once saying how he dreaded to see a woman running bare-headed: "It's a sure sign someone has died."

Perhaps there was something like that behind these acts of great intimacy and tenderness done to Jesus. Love, of course, but also feelings of fear and sorrow and loss. On each of these two quite different occasions, Jesus alone seems to have sensed the women's helpless desperation – what can you do in the face of so much that is wrong? And it may be they were the only ones to perceive the peril in which he walked. They dried his feet with their hair for their own sake, and for his.

(November 2008)

The Bible is full of stories of marriage and inheritance, love and high drama! God moves in mysterious ways, and often in our mysterious ways. Rebekah's story is one example, which I see as a Drama in Three Acts.

Mother of Twins
Or "How A Woman's Devious Ways Protected God's Promise"

Act 1 – Betrothal (Genesis 24:1-67)
We first meet Rebekah with a jug on her shoulder, come to the well for water: "The girl was very fair to look upon, a virgin, whom no man had known" (Genesis 24:16). Abraham had sent his servant all the many miles back to his own country and kindred, to find a wife for his son Isaac. Rebekah meets the servant at the well, gives him water to drink, and offers to water the camels too. With impulsive generosity, she invites him to stay with her family – "Yes, there is straw, yes, plenty of fodder with us, (and) yes, a place to spend the night" – and then has to run off home to tell her mother what she had just done! (Genesis 24:25-28). She makes her own decisions, and without delay sets off on the long unknown journey to Abraham's family, to become Isaac's wife (Genesis 24:57-67). Isaac was forty when he married Rebekah; she probably twenty or younger, if we are to take these figures at their face value. (Genesis 25:20)

Act 2 – Birth (Genesis 25:19-34)
For twenty years she is barren, and when she finally does conceive it leads to a difficult pregnancy. Not one to suffer in silence, Rebekah *"went to inquire of the LORD"*, and the Lord's answer was – twins!
Two nations are in your womb,
and two peoples born of you shall be divided;
the one shall be stronger than the other,
the elder shall serve the younger. (Genesis 25:19-28)

God confided in her, not in her husband Isaac. Like Hagar and her son Ishmael, Rebekah got her own promise, and she will cherish it. Two boys were born, rivals from the womb: Esau the first, but Jacob clinging to his heel even in the act of birth. *"When the boys grew up, Esau was a skilful hunter, a man of the field, while Jacob was a quiet man, living in tents. Isaac loved Esau, because he was fond of game, but Rebekah loved Jacob"* (Genesis 25:27-28).

Act 3 – Blessing (Genesis 27:1-40)
Many more years have passed. Isaac is now old and feeble and blind, and

it is time he gave his blessing to his son and heir. Heir, that is, not only to Isaac's considerable fortune but to the promise God made to Abraham that *"it is through Isaac that offspring shall be named for you"* (Genesis 21:12). It's the lineage that is in question: Abraham, Isaac – Who? Which of the twins is the heir? By right it ought to be Esau, the first-born and Isaac's choice. But Rebekah thinks otherwise as she recalls God's promise made to her: *the elder shall serve the younger.* Esau had already sold his birthright (Genesis 25:29-34), but that wouldn't mean anything if he got his father's blessing.

Rebekah does not wait for God to intervene to protect the promise. She takes matters into her own hands, or rather the hands of her favourite, Jacob. In a notorious con job on a blind man, she covers Jacob's hands with animal skins to make them feel like those of Esau, for as Jacob himself said, *"my brother is a hairy man, and I am a man of smooth skin"*. They got away with it and stole the blessing, to the terror of Isaac and the grief of Esau. We are not told what God might have felt about it.

It's a fine story, and could make a good play or film; for all I know it might already have done so. But why don't you read it for yourself, the complete version, including what happened to Esau and Jacob in later life? It is all there in the Book of Genesis. Read it for the story's sake!

(June 2009)

Mother of twins: a batik from Burkina Faso, West Africa.

I imagine a decent man, not involved in the hostile questioning of Jesus, Mark 11:27 – 12:27. I imagine Jesus delighted at an honest question, and encouraged by the scribe's interest and approval. We need more people like that!

A Very Jewish Answer

One of the scribes came near and heard them disputing with one another, and seeing that he answered them well, he asked him, "Which commandment is the first of all?"
(Mark 12:28-34)

"I will tell you of the time I met Jesus of Nazareth. As a scribe, I had a professional interest in this young man up from Galilee; so had all the other teachers and leaders in Jerusalem. He offended them, that's the only way to put it, so they ganged together to argue with him – an unlikely assortment of Pharisees and scribes and Sadducees and lackeys of King Herod. They took him on one by one and asked him trick questions which he easily answered; that angered them even more. For myself, I was more curious than hostile, but there was something I wanted to ask him.

"Finally I got my chance, and put my question to him – not a very original one, I'm afraid: 'Which is the greatest commandment? What is it we must do?' He remained silent for a little while. We all waited, and then, quite softly, Jesus began to pray – at least that's what I thought he was doing: *'Hear, O Israel: the Lord our God, the Lord is one; you shall love the Lord your God with all your heart...'* I found myself joining in the prayer. *'...with all your soul, and with all your strength.'* The *Shema*, the prayer we Jews recite every day: the daily reminder of the centre and direction of our lives.

"I was about to speak when he turned to me and continued: *The second is this, 'You shall love your neighbour as yourself.' There is no other commandment greater than these.* He was so sure of this, almost fierce about it. In answer to my old chestnut of a question he had taken a phrase from Leviticus about loving your neighbour, and laid it down beside the prayer from Deuteronomy about loving God, and it caught fire! It was a very Jewish answer.

"I found myself liking this man, rough and ready as he seemed at times. What he said was right, and I told him so. These commandments were not so much a rule as a response to the One Who is One; they could not be separated, how we stand with God and how we stand with our neighbour. Getting that right, I said, was more important than any sacrifice we might offer. I think the prophets had the sense of it long ago; as Hosea put it, *For I desire steadfast love and not sacrifice, / the knowledge of God rather than burnt offerings.*

"He seemed a bit surprised at my reaction, and pleased. He'd been having a hard time of it from so many who opposed him that to meet someone who even half understood what he was saying must have been an encouragement, an affirmation. The truth is he didn't have much time for scribes, nor they for him. But he stared at me – I can picture it to this day – and nodded

Batik from Nigeria – two Fulani men talking.

and said, 'You are not far from the kingdom of God.'

"I never met him again, and a short time later he was crucified. I try to live by what he said that day; I believe his teaching came from the Torah, our Jewish Law. But I have not felt able to join his followers – I fear it is a step too great for me. So I stand here, not far from the 'kingdom of God' as he said, hoping that 'not far' is near enough."

(See Leviticus 19:18; Deuteronomy 6:4-9; Hosea 6:6)

(March 2010)

Huldah lived in Jerusalem at a time of a disastrous decline in faith. Most rulers were corrupt; only Josiah tried to recover and renew faith in the God of Israel. Then they discovered the lost "Book of the Covenant." I leave Huldah to tell her story of what happened then. I think we today might learn something from what Huldah has to say. Read 2 Kings Chapters 21 to 23. 640-586 BC

Huldah's Wisdom

"I will wipe Jerusalem as one wipes a dish,
wiping it and turning it upside down."
(2 Kings 21:13)

"My name is Huldah, and I am a prophet. Before it was all torn down I lived with my husband Shallum in the Second Quarter of Jerusalem. And it was there they brought me a book they had found while repairing the Temple; they thought it might be the lost Book of the Covenant. They were frightened men that day, I tell you!

"Josiah was a good man and a good king, very different from those who had gone before him. He had inherited a mess, a kingdom broken by both the Assyrian invaders and his own royal ancestors – a sorry lot, generally! Perhaps that is why he appreciated the workers he had brought in to repair the Temple; as he put it, "They deal honestly". And so it was that, somewhere in the rubble and dirt, they discovered the book. Whether it was truly lost-and-found, or had been written-and-hidden by some group of scholars, I could not say. But the King was shocked when they read it to him, and wanted to know if it were genuine. So he sent it to me. I am a prophet; I know the Word of God when I hear it, even if I do not know how it came to be there. God's Word was there, in the book.

"I sent two messages back to the king. The consequences of our failures, I said, would continue to unfold; nothing would stop that now. But for himself, he should finish what he had set out to do. He saw the evil that had taken root among us, he acknowledged where he himself had failed and did not try to hide the wrong done by other kings and leaders.

"He did what good leaders do, what Joshua had done at Shechem and Moses had done at Sinai: he took the people into his confidence. He gathered all the elders and priests and prophets, all the people both small and great, and laid it out before us. He read in our hearing all the words of the book of the covenant which had been found in the house of the Lord. And there in the Temple, the king renewed the covenant with God, and all the people joined

106

in the covenant. It was as if we had found ourselves again and remembered who we were.

"Then we set to work, and it was a hard, bitter work. There was so much to be won back; so much that was warped and wrong. So much hurt: you know, they had been burning children in the valley of Ben-Hinnom, can you imagine? That's how far we had fallen away!

"What happened then? Well, the world happened then: while we were gathering the fragments of our own ruin, greater forces were on the move. The Egyptians surged up from the south and overran us at Megiddo, that was where Josiah was killed. And after a few years, the Babylonians arrived and finished us off. They did what neither Egypt nor Assyria was ever able to do: they destroyed

Batik image of Jerusalem.

Jerusalem – Temple, walls, houses, schools, markets, everything. What I had prophesied came to pass.

"I'm old and tired, and maybe I've seen too much. We're nowhere near the end yet. Still, what Josiah did gives me hope. He was neither priest nor prophet, but he made us face truths we had long turned away from, and he faced them himself. I dread to think how much worse our condition might be now, if that had never happened."

(September/October 2010)

This reflection on Angels is a walk on the wild side. It was suggested by the batik from Burkina Faso in West Africa, and by the Feast of the Annunciation, March 25th. Angels are reliable messengers, but also come from the wild side.

Annunciations

In the sixth month the angel Gabriel was sent by God to a town in Galilee called Nazareth.
(Luke 1:26-38, Feast of Annunciation, March 25th)

Angels are messengers; but do they have wings? In the making of the Ark of the Covenant, the craftsman Bezalel *"made two cherubim of hammered gold... the cherubim spread out their wings above, overshadowing the cover with their wings"* (Exodus 37:7-9). Some texts in the Bible imply that angels can fly (Psalm 91:11-12; Daniel 14:33-39; Luke 16:22), and centuries of pictorial art have settled the image in our minds – angels have wings: that's how you know they are angels! The Irish poet W. B. Yeats has *The Mother of God* recalling,
> *Wings beating about the room;*
> *The terror of all terrors that I bore*
> *The Heavens in my womb.*

And yet when Tobias went to find a companion for the journey from Nineveh to Ecbatana, he "found the angel Raphael standing in front of him; but he did not perceive that he was an angel of God." He looked like a young man – in fact, a young man in a hurry: *"All right, I will wait; but do not take too long"* (Tobit 5:4-8). To tell the women that Jesus had risen from the dead, Mark has a *"young man, dressed in a white robe"* at the empty tomb; Luke has *"two men in dazzling clothes."* Matthew however decides it is *"an angel of the Lord, descending from heaven... whose appearance was like lightning, and his clothing white as snow"* (Mark 16:5-7; Luke 24:4; Matthew 28:2).

So in what guise did the angel Gabriel appear to Mary? Luke does not say, but when I saw this batik from Burkina Faso in West Africa, I wondered if Gabriel too might have been a *"young man"*: a farmer, say, coming in from the fields with his hoe and his harvest, who met the girl with a bundle of firewood on her head, and spoke to her the message he had been given to carry. And to her own abiding astonishment she answered "Yes!" while a woman winnowing grain witnessed the encounter, and the wind carried the chaff away as it were a wind from God sweeping over the face of the waters (Genesis 1:2).

Batik from Burkina Faso, West Africa.

Luke did not witness the Annunciation, any more than the artists and poets of later times. He wrote about 85 AD, long after the time of Jesus' birth, and even of his death and resurrection. His language was drawn from the Jewish scriptures, and from the preaching of the early Church – *Jesus, the Most High, the Lord God, throne of David, Holy Spirit, Son of God.* Paul had done as much thirty years earlier in his letter to the Romans: *"the gospel concerning his Son, who was descended from David according to the flesh, and was declared to be Son of God with power according to the Spirit of holiness"* (Romans 1:3-4).

Luke does not tell us what the Annunciation "looked like", rather what it means for us. The message given to Gabriel to carry says two things: the child to be born of Mary will be the Messiah, a son of the House of David; and he will be the Son of God. This is the Gospel, and Mary will follow it: *"Let it be with me according to your word."* It was a word she would keep all her life (see Luke 8:21).

Angels are spirits and, strictly speaking, have no need of age or gender or bodies. To suit us, however, they may come on wings or on agricultural earth, in a hurry or by stealth, as a stranger or as a familiar friend. They carry messages, and they require an answer.

(March 2011)

Another voice from the story of Israel, when the chosen people were still new to the Promised Land. Around 1220 BC. Judges 4 & 5; also Deuteronomy 16:18-20.

Mammy's Boy

"I will surely go with you; nevertheless, the road on which you are going will not lead to your glory, for the Lord will sell Sisera into the hand of a woman."
(Judges 4:9)

"I'm sitting under my palm tree. I am a judge, and I've spent so much time holding court here they've named it 'The Palm of Deborah'. I am also a prophet, as the Lord wishes. I am married to Lappidoth, and we live near Bethel in the hill country of Ephraim. And once, I went to war; it was being a prophet got me into that.

"For twenty years King Jabin of Canaan had been harassing us. The Israelite tribes were weak and divided, but the Lord told me to send Barak into battle; Sisera, the commander of the king's army, was the man to beat. Barak was a brave soldier but a bit of a mammy's boy too, he wanted me to hold his hand for him: 'If you will not go with me, I will not go!' I asked did he want a woman to

"He asked for water and she give him milk." (Judges 5:25) Painting on canvas of a milk seller in Nigeria. Artist: M. Oladoja

get the credit, but he insisted I come with him. Only a few of the tribes supported us, but we went to war anyway, and we won. Or, to be honest, the Lord won, as at the Red Sea and in much the same way: the heavens opened, and a flash-flood in the river Kishon destroyed their iron chariots. We wiped out Sisera's army, but not Sisera!

"Surprisingly, Sisera turned out to be a mammy's boy also. Everyone was afraid of him when he led a great army with chariots and weapons – big man, big mouth! And his mother, waiting for him at home, liked him to bring her embroidered scarves from the spoils of war. But once he knew he was going to be beaten, he ran away: jumped down from his chariot, and slipped through the confusion of the fighting. Left his men to their fate.

"And that was how I got my own comeuppance! When I had prophesied to Barak that a woman might take the glory away from him, I was thinking of myself. How wrong I was! Sisera ran till he arrived at the tent of Heber and his wife Jael. He was exhausted, and Jael invited him in, put him lying down, covered him with a blanket and gave him a drink of milk as you would a tired child. Then she killed him. Don't ask – you don't want to know!

"Eventually Barak and his men arrived in hot pursuit, and Jael showed them the body. And that was the end of the campaign. Of course, they wrote a song about it all: "When locks are long in Israel". Well, it wasn't just the warriors untying their hair as they went into battle, but loosening the bonds of oppression. We all get a mention in the song: I, Barak, Sisera – and his mother! Even the stars in the heavens have a part to play. But the real star is Jael:

> He sank, he fell,
>   he lay still at her feet;
> at her feet he sank, he fell:
>   where he sank, there he fell dead.

"Well, that battle is over now, and for a while at least there should be peace. We're not all that long in this country, and sometimes I worry about our place here. And like any mother, I worry about what my children may have to face in the future. But I am also a judge, under my palm tree, and I remember a thing Moses said to judges and other officials in the tribes: *'Justice, and only justice, you shall pursue, so that you may live and occupy the land the Lord your God is giving you.'* I think that's the real battle we have to win."

(May 2011)

The story of Saul is a tragic one; he did not cope well with being a king, and David outshone him completely. Yet, Saul inspired great loyalty and affection. Here I imagine how three people remember him.

Death of a King

When the people of Jabesh in Gilead heard what the Philistines had done to Saul, the bravest men started out and marched all night to Beth Shan. They took down the bodies of Saul and his sons from the wall, brought them back to Jabesh, and burnt them there. Then they took the bones and buried them under the tamarisk tree in the town, and fasted for seven days.
(I Samuel 28:1 – II Samuel 1:27)

The Witch at Endor: "Saul asked me to raise the dead: it was my skill. He had been such a handsome man; now he was pitiable. He had never been a match for David, his best warrior. And the foolish women's chanting hadn't helped: Saul has slain his thousands, / and David his ten thousands. What did they think Saul the King would make of that? But now Saul was desperate: he had alienated David; Samuel the prophet had died; God wouldn't talk to him; and the Philistine army was massed against him. Even though he had banished witches and wizards from the land, in the end he came to me – to raise the ghost of Samuel.

"Well, I raised Samuel for Saul, for all the good it did him. The prophet, who had never liked him anyway, spoke bluntly: Saul had been rejected, and the kingdom given to David. Saul and his sons would die on the morrow. The Philistines would win. Just like that. With nothing left to hope for, Saul left my house and went into the dark night. A poor brave man."

King David: "I know there are some who will never forgive me for Saul, but he was my hero too, my mentor. From the day of Goliath I was his man. I came to know his moods and his fears; he was a brave man, and a fine soldier, but being king was too much for him. He had neither the cunning nor the patience for it. I have, and so I was a threat to him. Saul was a ploughman and I was a shepherd: they don't always mix well. In the end he drove me away.

"Jonathan was his favourite son, fearless and gentle. And Saul was afraid I would take Jonathan from him. But as it turned out, they fought side by side on Mount Gilboa.
Saul and Jonathan, beloved and lovely!
In life and in death they were not divided.

The
Witch
and the
King;
batik from
Nigeria.

And I wasn't there to help them. The story is that when Saul knew all was lost, and had seen his three sons killed, he took his own life. But who knows what happens in the thick of battle? Whatever happened, the Philistines cut off Saul's head, stripped off his armour, gathered the bodies, and fastened them to the walls of Beth Shan for all to see.

How are the mighty fallen,
and the weapons of war perished!

A Man of Jabesh: "Ah, Saul! My dear, dead king! We set off that night from Jabesh to Beth Shan, running and marching. A full night's journey, across Jordan river, right into enemy territory. Nobody tried to stop us. Even the Philistine garrison at Beth Shan knew better than to mess with us. We took the poor, hacked bodies from the walls of the town and carried them home. We mourned them at Jabesh, and buried them with honour. We paid our debt.

"You see, many years earlier, when the Ammonites tried to destroy us, Saul forced the other tribes to come to our defence. In the spirit of God, he chopped up the oxen he was ploughing with, and sent the pieces around the country – Come to help us, or I'll do the same to you! Hah! It frightened the wits out of them. But they came, thousands of them, and we beat the Ammonites back. King Saul saved us; we've never forgotten him for it."

(November 2011)

113

5: Liturgy & Seasons

The Gate of Heaven

St Hilary refers to "the Creator, the Only-Begotten, and the Gift". So I wondered what this Nigerian batik might tell us.

Batik Trinity

"The grace of the Lord Jesus Christ, the love of God, and the fellowship of the Holy Spirit be with you all."
(2 Corinthians 13:13)

Sometimes, if the quality of the yarn makes it worthwhile, you can unpick the threads of a garment in order to knit them together again in a different pattern. This batik from Nigeria reminds me of that possibility, wondering what the artist, Nike Davies Okundaye, had in mind. What questions was she asking about the Trinity, what patterns was she knitting together? Somehow I think questions are as much as we can ever hope to get about God *"who is able to do so much more than we can ask for, or even think of"* (Ephesians 3:20). But there might be some patterns, some echoes of God's great reality.

The batik has many ambiguities: is that an infant or an adult? A baby to be wrapped in swaddling cloths and laid in a manger, or a dead body to be wrapped in linen cloths and laid in a tomb? (Luke 2:7; 23:53). Are the arms stretched out in desire, or in death? Is that a royal crown, or a crown of thorns – honour or shame? The hosts of angels crowding close: are they singing "Holy, Holy, Holy", or are their mouths and eyes rounded with horror at what they see? Indeed, there was much that was horrible in the life and death of God's Son, once he was left at our mean mercy.

And the magnificent dove with a wingspan as wide as a man's reach – think what a wind those wings would stir, should they begin to beat. And, yet, here the artist has placed the dove lower than the angels and the human. That is not how we usually image the Spirit that hovered over the waters at the creation (Genesis 1:2), and who descended upon Jesus at his baptism (Luke 3:21-22). Perhaps that is what Nike intends, that this Divine Presence lives at our level, not at a distance but within the inmost spaces of our lives. *"The Spirit of God is within you"* (I Corinthians 3:16). That's a hefty thought!

There is another pair of outstretched arms, violet and dark, behind the head of the man/child. Is that all we see of the Father in this batik Trinity? Is that all we need to see: arms flung wide in sympathy, suffering with the Son? *"Whoever has seen me has seen the Father"* (John 14:9). And we have seen the Son on a cross, as he "stretched out his arms between heaven and earth in the everlasting sign of God's covenant" (Eucharistic Prayer I for Masses of Reconciliation).

An unusual representation of the Holy Trinity in this batik from Nigeria.

It is this pattern of outstretched arms, and wings, that intrigues me most. It echoes down through the ancient scriptures and in the story of God's People: that they were saved from slavery *"with signs and wonders, with mighty hand and outstretched arm"* (Deuteronomy 4:34; Jeremiah 32:21; Psalm 136:12). And, yet, it may be that Nike's batik has another message; that she is knitting the threads into a different pattern. What does it mean when you open wide your arms? Probably that you want to hug someone – to welcome, to end a long absence or a falling out, to hold someone whose pain you cannot diminish but which you can share. It is a gesture of giving and of love and of gathering in. It's what we do at our best. And Nike's batik Trinity suggests that it is typical of God.

(May 2004)

The words we use at the Consecration in the Eucharist go back to the first Century and the memory of the Last Supper. Amazingly, what we do, the actions we perform, are just as old. There is great stamina in our liturgy!

The Things We Do

He took bread and gave you thanks;
he broke the bread, gave it to his disciples...
Eucharistic Prayer

I'm having great difficulty praying for this new pope! After twenty-six years of repeating "your servant Pope John Paul" in the Eucharistic Prayer of every Mass I celebrated, the groove has worn very deep: the mind glides along the familiar, and suddenly I'm having to correct myself, in a panic to recall the new name. The parishioners rightly conclude I'm past it.

Familiarity is the big danger; it is easy to miss the meaning of the things we do. It was not only what Jesus said at the Last Supper that was handed down, but also what he did. And I, mostly unaware, for the past forty years have been mimicking, imitating what Jesus did that night – that he took bread, blessed, broke the bread, and gave it to his companions. Four actions, four things that he did, and that I now do as a priest.

He took bread – the simplest of gestures, a necessary action in the sequence of consuming food: take, put in your mouth, chew, swallow. No big deal. Except for the wonder that the Son of God took anything at all – bread, wine, flesh, blood, skin, hunger, friendship, family, life, death...In a word, incarnation: entangling the life and living of humanity; embedded in creation, taking what already belongs to him.

He blessed, said the blessing, thanked. The tradition varies, whether you would say that Jesus "blessed" or "gave thanks". There is little difference – the background is the Jewish practice of blessing God for created things: "Blessed are you, Lord, God of all creation, through your goodness we have this bread to offer..." They blessed God, not the food and drink: it is another way of thanking – and of thinking.

He broke the bread – again, the simplest thing: to make sharing possible. Bread broken in order to unite: *"Because there is one bread, we who are many are one body, for we all partake of the one bread"* (1 Corinthians 10:17). Yet, so significant an action that, from the beginning, the Eucharist was known as "the breaking of bread".

Gave it to his disciples, as any host might do. They shared the one loaf; though as to the wine, it was not the usual thing, in that time and place, that all at table would share the same cup – for Jesus to give his own cup for others to drink was exceptional. Those who have communion with him in this meal share in the sacrifice by which he saved the world: "... by your Holy Spirit gather all who share this one bread and one cup into the one body of Christ, a living sacrifice of praise" (Eucharistic Prayer IV).

I can – and do – forget this, much of the time, and without attention go through the motions of what is given to me to say and to do. The words and deeds of Jesus and the memories of the early Church are stored in the Gospels and the writings of the New Testament. Stored also in the way we pray and worship: the liturgy of the Church is very tenacious. Despite the many changes and adaptations over the centuries, we still break the bread and drink the wine of our salvation. And now, too, we pray for "your servant Pope Benedict" – that is another long tradition we hold to in our Eucharist.

A food seller from West Africa balances two bowls on her head, and carries a drinking bowl in her hand in this batik from Burkina Faso.

(November 2005)

117

Body Count

The Lord's is the earth and its fullness,
the world and all its peoples.
(Psalm 24:1)

In the Catholic liturgical calendar the month of November opens with two remarkable days, both of them having to do with dead people. The "saints" of All Saints Day are, by definition, dead – in the early Church their veneration began at their tombs, and their feastday is traditionally their *natale*, their birthday into heaven. And the "souls" of All Souls Day are "those who have died in the peace of Christ and all the dead whose faith is known to you alone" (Eucharistic Prayer IV).

In *The Twentieth Century Book of the Dead*, Gil Elliott chronicles most of the wars and disasters of the last century, the bloodiest century ever. Among other things, he draws attention to the way the dead were counted, particularly those killed in warfare: 1,572 soldiers, 50,000 civilians; 29,638 military personnel, civilians: unknown, possibly several million. The military counts its casualties, it estimates for civilians. At least, that is the presumption: the army knows its own; round figures for the rest – and the rest are so many!

The Book of Revelation, the Apocalypse, may have a similar body count. In its visions, as in the army, there are some precise figures:
"From the tribe of Zebulun twelve thousand,
from the tribe of Joseph twelve thousand,
from the tribe of Benjamin twelve thousand sealed."

In all, twelve thousand from each of the twelve tribes of Israel, making a total of 144,000 who were "sealed" for Christ. But that exact and significant figure is followed, as in the army, by an estimate: *"After this I looked, and there was a great multitude that no one could count, from every nation, from all tribes and peoples and languages, standing before the throne and before the Lamb, robed in white, with palm branches in their hands"* (Revelation 7:1-10).

The ways of counting the bodies are strangely alike, yet there is a difference: the army is dealing with death, the Apocalypse with life. All Saints and All Souls are indeed about dead people, some of them known and loved and honoured in our memory. But we celebrate their life, not their death – theirs, and all that great multitude whose names are long forgotten, their faith and their failings known to God alone: the unlisted and the lost, the unidentifiable in mass graves, the unborn who never saw the light of any day. In our Eucharist we declare that Christ's blood was shed *"for you and for all"*. It would be a pity to belittle or diminish that hope.

I have more: we count two thousand years since the time of Jesus, but what of the two million years since humans first began to emerge on this planet? What of the human lives that developed then and since then, do they not also fall within the mercy of God? This is not a new thought: the Apostles' Creed has it that Jesus "descended to the dead" – it used to be "descended into hell" – to lead out, as it was believed, all those who from Adam's time on were awaiting the coming of the Saviour. They called it "The Harrowing of Hell". It's a quaint notion, yet I tend to believe in it, and in what it says about God's vast love for *"the world and all its peoples"* (Psalm 24:1).

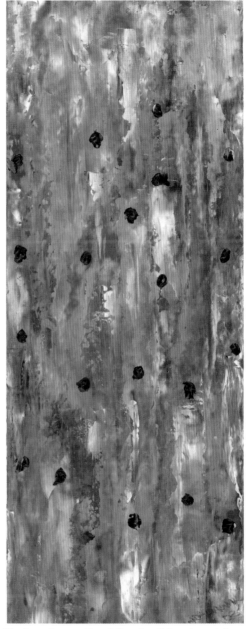

"Audience": an oil painting by Taiwo Lawal from Nigeria.

(November 2006)

119

We not only count our dead; we remember them in honour and affection. And it is a strong desire within us that we preserve their names.

A Wall of Names

In its original design, the **Vietnam Veterans Memorial** in Washington DC in the USA is formed by two tapering walls of black reflective granite, seventy-five metres long, set at an angle and struck into the earth like the blade of a plough. On the walls are etched the names of all the members of the U.S. armed forces who were killed in that war. Long after the memorial was dedicated in 1982, thousands of people still come every day, to find the names, sometimes to touch them or kiss them, or to leave small tributes of flowers or ribbons or other mementoes at the base of the walls.

There were other slaughters in the twentieth century, and other war memorials and lists of names, in cities and small towns and market-places, on the walls of churches and civic buildings in many countries. They too give the names, and sometimes the age and rank, of the fallen. Heroic or tragic statuary can impress – and some was added to the original starkness of the Memorial Wall in Washington – but a name is closer to the heart than any statue; a name makes connections. A wall of names is a chorus of meeting and remembering, though many memorials are from so long ago now that few recognise the names any more.

Sometimes the remembered names cannot be seen but rather are heard. The **Yad Va Shem Holocaust Memorial** in Jerusalem honours the almost six million Jews who died at the hands of the Nazis in the Shoah. "And to them will I give in my house and within my walls **a memorial** and **a name** [**yad** *va* **shem**] that will never be cut off" (Isaiah 56:5). In the Children's Memorial, all the Jewish children who perished in the death camps are remembered: endlessly and without remission, their names, ages and places of origin are recited over and over again, in a dark space lit only by a few candles reflecting like stars in sheets of glass. *"The human spirit is the lamp of the Lord"* (Proverbs 20:27). Over and over and over their names are spoken into the darkness, carried on a wall of sound.

Eucharistic Prayer I, the Roman Canon, is the most densely populated of all the Prayers; it contains more names and refers to more people, past and present. Here are angels and patriarchs – Abel, Abraham, Melkizedek; the Pope and bishop of our time and place; the living and the dead. And uniquely there are two lists of apostles and martyrs, two walls of names etched on the fabric of the Prayer, headed by "the glorious and ever-Virgin Mary, mother of our God and Lord, Jesus Christ."

Dying a martyr's death is not necessarily the same as a soldier dying on the field of battle, but they do share some things. The same pain and horror and agony, the same loss and sundering from their families and living friends, the same desolation and pride among those who are bereft of their love and laughter. Neither martyrdom nor being killed in action come cheaply, down to our own day.

The names of the martyrs in the Roman Canon have lost their charge of grief, and are remembered as saints. But the liturgy goes farther than that. As the new translation has it, in the Mass we are "in communion with those whose memory we venerate." Not only the martyrs and saints, but the whole Church, including those "who have gone before us with the sign of faith and rest in the sleep of peace." We don't just remember them; we are in union with them, as we are with Christ, in praising the wonders of God's works. I suppose, in a sense an amount of that happens at the Memorial Wall too. But we are never so near our dead as we are when celebrating the Eucharist.

Mary
Joseph
Peter
Paul
Andrew
James
John
Thomas
James,
Philip
Bartholomew
Matthew
Simon
Jude
Linus
Cletus
Clement
Sixtus
Cornelius
Cyprian
Lawrence
Chrysogonus
John
Paul
Cosmas
Damian
John the Baptist
Stephen
Matthias
Barnabas
Ignatius
Alexander
Marcellinus
Peter
Felicity
Perpetua
Agatha
Lucy
Agnes
Cecilia
Anastasia

These are the names of saints and martyrs as commemorated in the Roman Canon.

(May 2009)

A very brief overview of the composition of the New Testament, a collection of writings from the hundred years after the death and resurrection of Jesus.

Four for a Boy

There are four corners on my bed,
there are four angels overhead.
Matthew, Mark, Luke and John:
God bless the bed that I lie on.
(Bedtime Nursery Rhyme)

It is possible that the first written testimony to Jesus Christ was that penned by Pontius Pilate and fixed to the cross: *Jesus the Nazarene, the King of the Jews* (John 19:19; and Matthew 27:37; Mark 15:26; Luke 23:38). This, however, was no more than the charge laid against him, and in any case Pilate is an unreliable witness.

We are on safer ground with St Paul when, about twenty-five years later, he wrote down what he himself had been taught: *that Christ died for our sins in accordance with the scriptures, and that he was buried, and that he was raised on the third day in accordance with the scriptures* (I Corinthians 15:3-4). One of the earliest biographical references to Jesus, this passage says two things. First, that the Christian message is based on a real-life event – the life, death and resurrection of Jesus Christ. Second, that all that was done in Christ was in accord with the Jewish scriptures, our "Old Testament". Hold on to that thought!

Over the next one hundred years, as the teaching about Jesus spread, more and more was being written about him. Eventually there were so many versions that the early Christians had to sort out what was authentic and necessary, and what was simply helpful – or perhaps not. To put it another way, the Church needed to discern which writings carried authority. In the end we had our own book, which we call the "New Testament". It contains a variety of writing – letters, narrative, sermons, apocalyptic visions, and the four "Lives of Christ" we know today: Matthew, Mark, Luke and John, to give them the names of the people traditionally credited with writing them. The "Gospels" – a word that means Good News.

Luke called his version *"an orderly account"* (Luke 1:3); so are all four Gospels: they have the shape of a "Life", even if they play fast and loose with the details and sequence of the story. They are records more of the faith of the early Christians than of the facts of Jesus' life. And that brings us back to the Jewish scriptures. It is a favourite phrase of Matthew, that Jesus "fulfilled" the prophets. Like St Paul, and the early Christians in general, he saw a continuity between the Jewish experience of God and the events of the life of Jesus. Luke has Jesus saying, *"everything written about me in the law of Moses, the prophets, and the psalms must be fulfilled"* (Luke 24:44).

The Jewish experience has its own validity and grace, and it continues to this day. But there was a child born to it at Bethlehem, *"a saviour, who is the Messiah, the Lord"* (Luke 1:11). The

Four birds: Batik from Nigeria.

words are Jewish, but it is the budding of a new growth. It was a blessed instinct that led the Church to retain the Jewish scriptures as part of its own sacred writings: hence the "Old Testament" and the "New Testament" in one "Bible".

Our hope as Christians is to encounter Jesus in our own journey through life, and in finding him to find faith in him. The Gospels have a part to play in that: *"Now Jesus did many other signs in the presence of his disciples, which are not written in this book. But these are written so that you may come to believe that Jesus is the Messiah, the Son of God, and that through believing you may have life in his name"* (John 20:30-31).

(April 2011)

A child's game in Galilee reminds us that what we most need is maybe a bit of attention, even Jesus needed attention.

Child's Play

**"We played the flute for you, and you did not dance;
we wailed, and you did not weep."**
(Children's song from Galilee, Luke 7:32)

The man on the bus was going on and on in telling some long story or other. I wasn't his only audience, of course, but as I was sitting beside him, I was responding to him in the way you do (or at least as I find myself doing!) – "Is that so? … Really, is that so! … Mmmm, is that so now?" Until, finally, he rounded on me and said, to the great amusement of everyone else, "Will you stop saying, 'Is that so?' Amn't I telling you so?" He felt frustrated, and I didn't know what to say.

People get frustrated when they feel their voice is not being heard. Terry Pratchett puts it another way in one of his novels: "Charity ain't giving people what you want to give, it's giving people what they need to get." I know what I want to give: my left-overs – or as they say here, "second-new" shirts and trousers, stuff I no longer wear, or money it won't break me to give away. That's safe. But charity means loving as well as giving, and often what people need most is a bit of attention.

Attention, recognition, respect. That costs, because I don't know where it may lead me, or what it may demand of me. Paying attention to others means letting them pay attention to me, letting them get to know me – that's a commitment. I know people who do pay attention and get involved; they hang in there with the hurts and the desolations. They give themselves, and pay a great price in doing so.

As the Gospel according to Luke points out, both the austere John the Baptist and the gregarious Jesus needed attention, but people did not always listen to them. Jesus was reminded of children's games in Galilee: *"We played the flute for you, and you did not dance; we wailed, and you did not weep"* (Luke 7:31-35). Child's play can be mysterious, but it carries its own truth. Jesus didn't know whether to laugh or cry!

Luke's Gospel describes another occasion when Jesus swung between laughter and tears: it was on his final journey to Jerusalem, when some of the religious leaders tried to stop the disciples singing his praises; he laughed at them – *"I tell you, if these were silent, the stones would shout*

124

Child's Play
– Osoupele
and Bealsede,
two children
from Bomadi
in Nigeria,
take part in
masquerade
dancing.
(Photo: K.
Flynn SPS)

out." And yet, shortly after that, when he saw the stones of the city itself, he burst into tears, *"because you did not recognise the moment of your visitation"* (Luke 19:36-44; 1:68 JB). It's child's play again: laugh or cry, Jesus needed attention. We all do.

(July/August 2001)

Songlines

"Though we are sinners, we trust in your mercy and love; do not consider what we truly deserve, but grant us your forgiveness."
(Eucharistic Prayer I)

They say that the original inhabitants of Australia could sing their way across the continent, naming and reciting places that were otherwise uncharted. There are similar "songlines" in the scriptures, themes and titles that track their way through the Bible. One of them began, as the Book of Exodus tells it, in a meeting between Moses and God on Mount Sinai, where God passed before him and proclaimed,
"The LORD, the LORD,
a God merciful and gracious,
slow to anger,
and abounding in steadfast love and faithfulness."
(Exodus 33:12 - 34:9)

It entered into the imagination of the Jewish people. The mother-mercy of God became a motif in psalms of sorrow (Psalm 86), and in songs of praise for the grandeur of creation (Psalms 103; 111; 145).
But you, God of mercy and compassion,
slow to anger, O Lord,
abounding in love and truth,
turn and take pity on me.
(Psalms 86:15)
The prophets took up the theme (Isaiah 54:4-10; Jeremiah 32:18), though it annoyed Jonah, who would have preferred a more vengeful God: *"I knew that you are a gracious God and merciful, slow to anger, and abounding in steadfast love, and ready to relent from punishing".* In spite of him, God excused the sinners of Nineveh, *"who cannot tell their right hand from their left, to say nothing of all the animals."* (Jonah 4)

The songline continues in Jesus who gave body to the tenderness of God, though there were Jonah-grumblers there too: "This fellow welcomes sinners and eats with them". So he told them stories about a God who searches for lost sheep and shoulders them home, who sweeps the house looking for lost pennies, whose heart goes out to the young lad lost and miserable (Luke 15). Jesus forgave, and he too made excuses for the wrong-doers: *"Father, forgive them; they do not know what they are doing"* (Luke 23:34). The same mother-mercy is remembered in Mary's Magnificat, *"the*

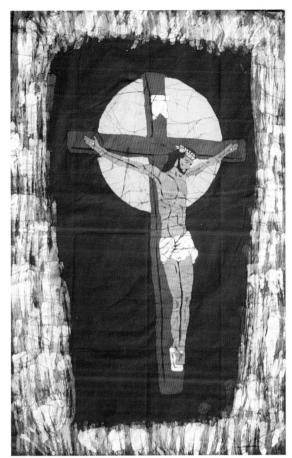

"Mindful of his mercy." This batik of the Crucifixion is from India.

mercy promised to our ancestors, to Abraham and his descendants for ever" (Luke 1:55).

There are three great monotheisms who claim descent from Abraham: Judaism, Christianity, and Islam. The songline of God's mercy is found in the faith of all three, for in the Qur'an too God says: "O my servants who have transgressed against themselves, despair not of the Mercy of God. For God forgives all sins, He is Oft-forgiving, Most Merciful" (39:53). And all but one of the 114 chapters of the Qur'an begin, "In the Name of God, Most Gracious, Most Merciful".

How is it that over centuries of conflict we, who are followers of these faiths, have found it so difficult to be merciful towards each other? *Kyrie eleison*, Lord have mercy!

(January/February 2007)

Jesus rose in the Springtime and we sing, Now the green blade riseth; if he had risen in November I wonder what hymns we would have sung.

A Winter's Tale

As for us, our days are like grass;
we flower like the flower of the field,
the wind blows and we are gone
and our place never sees us again.
(Psalm 103:15-16)

Leaves are amazing: they are the great power houses of trees. The upper side of a leaf, green with chlorophyll, collects energy from the light of the sun, much as solar panels do. The underside, filled with wet spongy tissue, is like a set of lungs, extracting carbon dioxide from the atmosphere and breathing out oxygen (our lungs do it the other way around, of course: oxygen in, carbon dioxide out). From all this, the leaf manufactures sugar energy packs, which are then shunted around the tree system as the fuel that keeps it growing.

But there is a downside. The large surface area of the leaf, so effective in the Summer light, becomes a liability in Winter – there is less sunlight, and the fragile leaves are too easily damaged by physical injury or freezing temperatures. The solution, for deciduous trees, is simple but risky: the leaves are made redundant and are laid off. The tree gives up its means of sustenance and energy, the leaves die, and fall to the ground. It is only in the Spring that fresh leaves are taken on, and the tree survives (Evergreens do it differently and keep their leaves, but that's another story).

The Springtime return of foliage has a resurrection quality to it; the dark turning of the year leads to light and a return of life. As the old Easter carol puts it, "Now the green blade riseth / from the buried grain."

But ours is a Winter's tale:
All flesh is grass
and all its beauty is like the flower of the field.
The grass withers, the flower fades
when the breath of the Lord blows upon it:
surely the people are grass.
(Isaiah 40:6-7)

I sometimes wonder had the death and resurrection of Jesus happened in the month of November what parallels in nature would we have found

Cassava leaves decorate a highly ornamented batik cloth from Nigeria.

to image them? And yet it is an old tradition in the Christian liturgy that we remember our dead in November. Was this a Northern Hemisphere thing, darkening days, skeletal trees, Winter's massive scything of life? Was it because November is a killing-field that we chose it to celebrate All Souls Day?

Letting go the leaves is a near-death experience for a tree. If for any reason the Spring days do not lengthen and warm sunlight return, the budding mechanism will not be triggered: there will be no new leaves, and the tree will die. There is an air of reckless hope about what the tree does, as we might ourselves feel when, in our grief, we let go our own at their time of dying: "Go forth, faithful Christian. May you live in peace this day."

Perhaps that is why we remember the dead in the terminal days of November, that we might nourish what hope we have, a hope more reckless than any in nature.

November 2004

6: Our World

The Work of Your Hands

Looking at this tabernacle sent me off on a long journey over time and space and matter and faith and people and all God had made: "and indeed, it was very good" (Genesis 1:31).

Real Presence

Father, you are holy indeed,
and all creation rightly gives you praise.
All life, all holiness comes from you
through your son, Jesus Christ, our Lord,
by the working of the Holy Spirit.
(Eucharistic Prayer III)

In 1972, an Irish artist, Ray Carroll, designed a tabernacle for St Brigid's Chapel at the Formation House for St Patrick's Missionary Society at Kiltegan, Co. Wicklow, Ireland. I knew Ray – he was a good man and a good artist, and he died in 1994 at the age of sixty-six. The pedestal of the tabernacle was made from a West African hardwood, and the tree it came from was possibly 100 years old when it was harvested. Years and ages have a meaning in all this.

Set into the face of the pedestal was a fossil fish, brought back from Brazil in 1973. In the hunted times of the early Church, the sign of a fish was a coded reference to Christ: the five letters of the Greek word for fish, I-CH-TH-U-S, seemed to spell (in Greek, of course) Jesus Christ God's Son Saviour. Jesus fed thousands of people with a few loaves and a couple of fish. A fish is a very appropriate symbol for a tabernacle. This fish is long extinct, and the fossil in St Brigid's is more than 100 million years old – it is part of the long story of life in our world.

There are iron nails and screws and clamps in the tabernacle and pedestal. Iron, any bit of iron, is older than the world – as flour is older than the bread made from it. As modern scientists describe it, many billions of years in the past, atoms of iron and other metals and heavy elements were forged by nuclear forces in the depths of the earliest stars and scattered like dust over vast stretches of time and space in gigantic stellar explosions. Eventually, the force of gravity clumped these particles of dust and atoms

and elements together to form new stars, among them our sun, and the planets and moons and asteroids of our solar system. They reckon that process was completed about four-and-a-half billion years ago: that's how old the earth is. Iron is older still and today we mine and smelt and refine this ancient metal, and make nails of it.

The door of the tabernacle of St Brigid's Chapel recalls the miracle of the loaves and fishes, while the 100-year-old fossil of an extinct species of fish found in Brazil adorns a panel in the tabernacle pedestal. (Photo: Kiltegan)

So, in our tabernacle we have the wonders of time, matter, life, and beauty, and the skill that brought them all together to contain – and yet not contain – the Presence of the One through whom all these things were made. A tabernacle is not just for storage, but to focus our hearts on a presence. Read your own heart, and you will know that the presence of the one you love is not a static thing; it is more like a dance, with movement and intimacy and completion.

Could it be that there is such a dance within the community of God: Father, Son, Spirit? Is this what Eucharistic Prayer III is saying? And that creation is caught into the dance – the world and its life, the wood of the tabernacle and the wood of the cross and the wood of the forest, any old iron, the skill and faith of the artist, and the assemblies of people at Eucharist who join Christ in acknowledging the works of God and in offering the sacrifice. Or am I imagining things?

(November 2001)

How recent are the scientific discoveries that describe our modern understanding of the world! Little more than a single lifetime ago we learned how old and how vast the Universe is.

Let it be!

When I look at your heavens, the work of your fingers,
the moon and the stars that you have established;
what are human beings that you are mindful of them,
mortals that you care for them?
(Psalm 8 NRSV)

About ten years before I was born (as recently as that!) the perception of the world we live in was radically changed. Cold dark skies on November nights in Ireland were my own introduction to the stars, the thousands (actually only about 2,000 at any one time) that are visible to the naked eye. The stars seemed so stable, unchanging, steady; they counted the years and the seasons, ships sailed by their guidance.

Then, in the 1920s, Edwin Hubble discovered that there is no stillness in the stars: the universe is in frightening motion, space is expanding, spreading wildly away from us. What had appeared to be dust, or very distant stars in our own *Milky Way* Galaxy, turned out to be other galaxies, billions of them, each containing billions of stars. The universe was older and larger than had ever been suspected: about fourteen

This batik from the African country of Burkina Faso depicts a man, who has just come from the farm with a hoe over his shoulder, reaching down to pick up his beloved child from the hands of his wife.

billion years, give or take, since it all came boiling out of the Big Bang. And as to *large*, you couldn't imagine! It is not, as had been thought, static and unchanging, fixed as God had made it. The universe has a story: "Creation – The Movie!"

It's an amazing narrative the astronomers have described – violent, destructive, inventive, and vast beyond comprehension. And tucked away in at least one small corner of it there is life, with its own tale billions of years long – even if the part humans have played is very, very brief. Otherwise, I wouldn't be here writing this, nor you reading it. But that's another story: let me stay with the stars. The blazing sky and the luxuriant earth have always provoked wonder and praise: *"Let the heavens rejoice and the earth be glad, let the sea and all within it thunder praise"* (Psalm 96). A God of Great Things.

But what can you say of the God that the *new* story of creation hints at? What kind of a God would make a world that grows and changes, makes choices, takes chances, forever flaring into new shapes and surprises? This is a God who doesn't just create the universe and settle it to its shape, but who allows it to grow and develop, to be and to become – as it is still doing. I might need to think about that for a while; it all sounds very risky, on a very grand scale! Does God really take chances?

I find myself falling back on an old Bible image (Hosea 11): maybe God is parenting the universe, like a father or mother teaching a child to walk, having to let go and allow the child to take its own steps. And, if there is a fall, isn't that part of the story too: the parent suffers when the child falls. Perhaps God, too, walks closely with creation, sustaining and enduring all that happens, and suffering with the world's falls and failures. Creation goes with compassion. Yes, I believe God does take chances – the author of Psalm 8 seemed to think so too. Do you think is God taking a chance on us? On you?

(November 2002)

Come with me on a journey of light from our nearest galactic neighbour, a journey of two and a half million years.

As far as Andromeda

Father, it is our duty and our salvation
always and everywhere to give you thanks
through your beloved Son, Jesus Christ.
He is the Word through
whom you made the universe,
the Saviour you sent to redeem us.
Eucharistic Prayer II

A trick question: how far can you see with the naked eye? We think of the tallest buildings and the highest mountains, a cloudless day and a clear horizon. But the fact is we can see farther in the dark: look up at the stars – they are billions of miles away.

Of all the objects in the night sky that can be seen with the naked eye, the farthest away is the Andromeda galaxy: so far away that its light takes roughly two and a half million years to travel to my eye. To put it another way, it is 2.5 million light-years away – a "light-year" being the distance light travels in one year at a speed of 186,000 miles a second. So "As far as Andromeda" is as far as the eye can see. That sounds like an enormous distance, and so it is; but in astronomical terms, compared to the size of the universe as we know it now, it is only as far as your neighbour's back yard.

Two and a half thousand years ago, around the time of the prophets and psalmists of Israel, the light from Andromeda had travelled 99.9% of its journey to my eye; winging its way across the vast reaches of space, it still had a distance to go! They had their own science in those days and various stories of creation. But they did sense the enormity within which we live:

Have you not known? Have you not heard?
Has it not been told you from the beginning?
Have you not understood from the
foundations of the earth?
It is (God) who sits above the circle of the earth,
and its inhabitants are like grasshoppers;

134

who stretches out the heavens like a curtain,
and spreads them like a tent to live in.
(Isaiah 40:21-22)

For them the wonder was not just the magnitude of God's creation, but the care with which it was made: a God of love and compassion, whose word is faithful and all his works to be trusted (Psalm 33:4). The creator and the saviour are one and the same.

For as the heavens are high above the earth
so strong is God's love for the God-fearing;
As far as the east is from the west
so far does he remove our sins.
(Psalm 103:11-12)

The distance between heaven and earth seemed the only fit measure for the mercy of God; and east to west was out of sight! Even then our measuring falls short.

The light from the Andromeda galaxy finally falls on my eye: it is a gigantic wheel of four hundred billion stars, but I see it as just a faint smear in the night sky – it is so far away! To my naked eye it is not impressive; it might even be a disappointment if I did not remember the Magi and the star that brought them to Bethlehem (Matthew 2:1-12). The light from Andromeda could do as much for me. *By God's word the heavens were made, by the breath of his mouth all the stars* (Psalm 33:6).

Stars of the Universe
depicted by
S. Awowo on adire batik
cloth from Nigeria.

(January/February 2006)

Water flows through our lives, for drinking, cooking, washing, for life itself. Equally it flows through the Scriptures and the life of Jesus.

The Water Carriers

He made the camels kneel down outside the city by the well of water; it was toward evening, the time when women go out to draw water. *(Genesis 24:11. Read Chapter 24 for the betrothal of Isaac and Rebekah)*

*T*hey are collecting water to bring to their homes. A woman helps a girl to raise a container: it is too heavy for one person alone to lift, but once in position she will be able to carry it. In a moment, she will rise and stride away, the water balanced on her head. She will be magnificent, with her poise and bearing, a favourite of tourist photos and documentary films. But don't be deceived: it is drudgery, tiring and time-consuming. Even children have

to do it, often before they go to school – they may have to walk for miles, and it must be done today, and tomorrow, and next-tomorrow…

Water is often scarce and always precious, never more so than in desert country. The Bedouin in the deserts of the Middle East make a distinction between well

Three women collect water in this batik from Togo, West Africa.

water and spring water: you can own a well, but no one can own a spring. A well is a manufactured thing, dug into the earth, which you can buy and control; a spring is a gift of God – "the tears in the eyes of the earth" – and nobody can be refused access to spring water.

Perhaps this was at the back of Jesus' mind as he chatted with a water carrier from Samaria at Jacob's Well (John 4). Never one to miss a pun or a play on words, when she tendered him well water, he offered her spring water in return: *"If you knew the gift of God, and who it is that is saying to you, 'Give me a drink', you would have asked him, and he would have given you living water."* Living water, spring water: in the original languages, the words are the same. And only a step to where he would lead her next: to *"a spring of water gushing up to eternal life."* Living water, spring water, water of life – the words are still the same, but his meaning is now complete.

Jesus seems to have loved water: to sail on, to fish in, to eat beside, to walk by, and even, on one occasion, to walk upon! Storms at sea didn't faze him, nor indeed deserts with no water at all. His life was awash with water stories: rains that make things grow, floods that knock houses, drink to satisfy all our thirsts, water to wash feet with, and spit that heals. And of course, the practical joke with which he started it all, when he turned water into a vintage wine. As neat a gift as ever you'll get at a wedding! (John 2:1-11)

In all this, Jesus stood in a long tradition. If you had a mind to, you could follow a river of water-talk from beginning to end of the Bible: from the water-opening of Creation (Genesis 1:6-10), to the dividing of the Red Sea (Exodus 14:21-22), to Ezekiel's vision of water flowing from the Temple in Jerusalem (Ezekiel 47), and the echo of that vision in the Bible's final book – *"the river of the water of life… flowing from the throne of God and of the Lamb"* (Revelation 22:1-2).

When the water carriers come home they may bring more than water. Rebekah brought a marriage proposal (Genesis 24). The Samaritan woman brought a gospel (John 4). Though the art of the West tends to favour a house, it is the tradition of the Eastern Churches that the Annunciation took place at a well. So what did Mary bring with her, as she carried the water home?

(June 2006)

Following on from **As far as Andromeda**... *(see page 134).*

Look Back Time

I have been crucified with Christ;
and it is no longer I who live,
but it is Christ who lives in me.
(Galatians 2:19-20)

Remember Andromeda? The galaxy of stars that is so far away that its light takes two and a half million years to reach us – 2.5 million light years away. Of course, that means that what we are seeing is actually the Andromeda Galaxy *as it was* all those many years ago, when the light left it. Not as it is *now*. A light year is a measure of *distance* (How far away?) but also of *time* (How long ago?).

The fact is that everything we see in the night sky belongs to the past. The supernova that brightens the skies today exploded thousands of years ago; but it is only when its light reaches us that we can become aware of that. The nearest star, our own Sun, is eight and a half light minutes away and ago. The next nearest, Proxima Centauri, is 4.2 light years away and ago. They call this, look back time. And, as I gaze at the sky with all its many pasts, it makes me wonder: what does now mean?

I have been distracted by these wonderings ever since the dramatic days of Holy Week and Easter and the faith-story we celebrated then. The fact is that everything we read in our Bible belongs to the past. At the heart of our Christian story stands Jesus of Nazareth, the Son of God and our Saviour. But that story, and the Gospels and writings that tell of it, come from

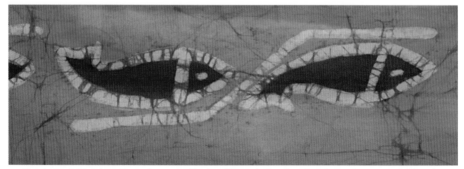

Symbols of Christ portrayed on a batik shawl from India; the shawl may be worn at Mass by the celebrant.

our past; and in our liturgies "we celebrate the *memory* of Christ, your Son" (Eucharistic Prayer I). What does now mean?

Jesus was a local hero. That's what Incarnation means: a flesh-and-blood-belonging to a particular people, place and time. Not to mention ending up  dead and buried, as the Creed tells us. Had it remained that way, what a sadness and wonder and charm his story would have held for us: good to look back to and to learn from, but dead and buried all the same.

Twenty-five years later, St Paul was writing that Jesus is alive: He was crucified in weakness, but lives by the power of God (2 Corinthians 13:4). That was the gospel from the very beginning: *The Lord has risen indeed, and he has appeared to Simon!* (Luke 24:34). The resurrection of Jesus was not a simple return to life-as-we-know-it, but broke the confines of time and space. The risen Lord is present to all ages and all times – in heaven and on earth and under the earth, as Paul sings (Philippians 2:10). No longer there and then, but always now.

There is no travel-time from Christ to us, no light years, no look back time. Maybe that's what *now* means: wherever and whenever Christ is present. I don't always live in the *now* of my life. I'm too often away, reliving the past or fearing the future or imagining elsewhere – but now is where I must meet him.

I think the liturgy, with its "memory of Christ your Son", is one of the now times of our lives, when we are washed and oiled and fed and touched and held by him. As if in order to live in the *now* we need some kind of touch, some sacrament of presence. Perhaps that is why Jesus still has a flesh-and-blood-belonging to a people: you are the body of Christ (1 Corinthians 12:27).

(September/October 2006)

Beasts and Saints

"Let them have dominion over the fish of the sea,
and over the birds of the air,
and over the cattle,
and over all the wild animals of the earth,
and over every creeping thing
that creeps upon the earth."
(Genesis 1:26)

Here is a playful drawing: how many animals can you count in it? It reminds me of the prophet Isaiah:
The wolf shall live with the lamb,
the leopard shall lie down with the kid,
the calf and the lion and the fatling together,
and a little child shall lead them. (Isaiah 11:6-8)
Animals of the wild at ease and peaceful with each other, though that is not their nature. Nor is it ours; Isaiah's vision belongs to a harmony we have yet to achieve.

There are endless stories of remarkable relationships between humans and animals: *Aesop's Fables*, Kipling's *Jungle Book*, all the beasts and saints that inhabit the legends of the Irish Monks and the Desert Fathers. Even *The Teddy Bears' Picnic*, although that song comes with warnings attached. We would have to disguise ourselves, or even the bears would run away from us! The truth is, humans have been hard on the other living creatures of our world; we are the deadliest animal of all.

I never liked circuses much. The trapeze and high-wire artistes, and the jugglers, I enjoyed; and even the sad madness of the clowns. But not the animals. Or rather, what they were made to do: tigers jumping through hoops of fire, elephants dancing to Strauss waltzes, animals dressed up in our clothes and aping human manners. It seemed lacking in respect for both animals and humans.

And yet, I am constantly amazed that even a townie like me can walk without worry through a herd of cattle: any one of them would be large enough to crush me easily. What is it we do to animals when we domesticate them? Is it that the only animals we can accept are those we have tamed or trained or slaughtered?

Assorted animals: an ink drawing from Nigeria.

According to the Genesis text, we were given dominion over the life of the earth; it has proved a difficult responsibility. But it is echoed in the *Prayer of Azariah* (Daniel 3) – the Genesis sequence is retraced, not in a "dominion over" but in a **celebration with** the creatures of the earth – there is greater humility in that, and more respect:

> *"Bless the Lord, you whales and*
> *all that swim in the waters…*
> *all birds of the air…*
> *all wild animals and cattle…*
> *all people on earth."*

(November 2007)

A Place of Springs

In your house I am a passing guest,
a pilgrim, like all my ancestors.
(Psalm 39:13)

Some years ago, in the heat of a long dry season in Nigeria, a friend sent me a photograph he had taken of Lough Tay in the Wicklow hills in Ireland. It is a place I know and love, not far from St Patrick's headquarters in Kiltegan. I was transported by the picture, by the contrast with the burnt landscape of my African surroundings, and a little heartsick for what the singer Tom Jones called *The Green, Green Grass of Home* – though he was thinking of Wales, not Ireland. Even now, whenever I look at this photograph my heart lifts.

For centuries before the time of Jesus there had been Jews living in exile in places like Egypt, Assyria and Babylon; it left traces in some of the psalms. Psalm 120, written out of the hostility of life in a foreign country: *Alas, that I abide a stranger in Meshech, / dwell among the tents of Kedar!* Or Psalm 137, with its exiles weeping by the rivers of Babylon: *O how could we sing / the song of the LORD / on alien soil?*

St Paul saw it differently: for him, home is a place we haven't been to yet. *"Our homeland is in heaven,"* he says (Philippians 3:20). We don't go back home. We are indeed exiles, en route, pilgrims, but to a place we have never seen. This is not a new thought; its roots are in the Exodus experience of the People of Israel, the 40-year trek through the desert from Egypt to the Promised Land – *"a land with fine, large cities that you did not build....vineyards and olive groves that you did not plant"* (Deuteronomy 6:10-12).

We are a pilgrim people, but what about the terrain we pass through on our journey? Our homeland may be in heaven, but this is the world we live in, this garden and valley-of-tears. Does God have a care for this world of ours? Should we? Listen to the Christian scriptures: *"For the creation waits with eager longing for the revealing of the children of God."* St Paul imagines that we, together with all creation, are being brought to birth by God (Romans 8). God will, in the fullness of time, *"gather up all things in (Christ), things in heaven and things on earth"* (Ephesians 1). This will be done for *"all things, whether on earth or in heaven, by making peace though the blood of his cross"* (Colossians 1). Yes, God cares.

A place of springs: Lough Tay, Co Wicklow (Photo: P Hardiman)

The scriptures speak their own language which is sometimes difficult to understand; modern science can also be difficult as it tells of Relativity, and Quantum Physics, and "dark" matter and energy. But both are reaching for the connectedness of "all things", the harmony of greatest and least, and the beauty, wonder, and hope of the world to which we belong.

Meanwhile the evidence gathers as to how endangered our world has become, partly due to our lack of care for it. Psalm 84, one of the great songs of journey and home, describes in the simplest way what the passage of a pilgrim people ought to mean for a desert:

They are happy, whose strength is in you,
in whose hearts are the roads to Zion.
As they go through the Bitter Valley
they make it a place of springs,
the autumn rain covers it with blessings.

(January/February 2010)

I begin a trilogy of reflections on our world, drawing on the Hebrew imagining of the kind of world we live in.

Water World – Part I

... darkness covered the face of the deep,
while a wind from God
swept over the face of the waters.
(Genesis 1:2)

When I was a child I fell into the pond in St Stephen's Green in Dublin, Ireland, Europe, Earth, The Universe. My father pulled me out and took me behind to the bushes where he could squeeze my short trousers dry, while someone else was minding the chairs we had hired for a shilling. It didn't mark any great change in my life; not like Pharaoh's daughter scooping the infant Moses out of the Nile, or Jesus steadying Peter on the waves of Lake Gennesaret till they could walk back to the boat together (Exodus 2:1-10; Matthew 14:22-36). But the fact remains that I was once drawn out of the waters of the pond in St Stephen's Green in Dublin, Ireland, Europe, Earth, The Universe.

I name my place in the Universe, as a child might do, because that's the scale of things with water in the Bible. As Genesis tells it, God first created light, and then a space in the primeval waters: *"Let there be a dome in the midst of the waters, and let it separate the waters from the waters"* (Genesis 1:1-10; Psalm 104:1-13). In this vision of things, we live in a bubble: spring water surges up from the Abyss beneath, and rain pours in through sluice-gates in the sky. Our world floats in the Deeps – Heaven above, and Hell below, and God above all as Fr Ned Grace shows in his painting:

> *Greater than the roar of mighty waters,*
> *More glorious than the surgings of the sea,*
> *The Lord is glorious on high.*
> (Psalm 93:4; 113:4-6)

But like any bubble, this one could burst. There came a time when *"all the fountains of the great deep burst forth, and the windows of the heavens were opened."* The Deeps came crashing into the living-space God had opened for us. Creation undone, with only Noah and his Ark spared to surf the waves (Genesis 7-9). "Flood" is too small a word for it: this could be Wipe out!

How we imagine Creation can shape the way we pray; there is a stream

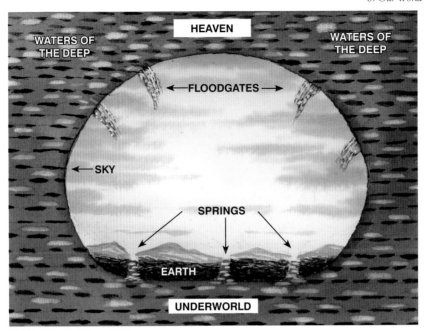

HEAVEN

WATERS OF THE DEEP

WATERS OF THE DEEP

←—FLOODGATES—→

←—SKY

SPRINGS

EARTH

UNDERWORLD

(Painting: Fr. Ned Grace SPS)

of water-talk that flows all through the psalms. *Save me, O God, / for the waters have come up to my neck… I have come into deep waters, and the flood sweeps over me* (Psalm 69:1-2, 13-15). When the need is immense, we use language as extreme as Creation. *Stretch out your hand from on high; / Set me free and rescue me from the mighty waters* (Psalm 144:7; 124:2-5; 148:1-4). The psalmist puts it simply:

> *Our help is in the name of the Lord,*
> *who made heaven and earth.*
> (Psalm 124)

Such was Creation-language long ago in Biblical times. But we know better now, and tell the narrative of our 13.7 billion-year-old universe in a different way. Yet traces of the old story persist: we get soaked when "the skies open"; we say the Sun rises and goes down; we devoutly pray "here below." And when Yuri Gagarin blasted into the heavens in April 1961, the first human to orbit in space around the globe, they asked him had he seen God! For all our new knowledge about the nature of our universe, we still accept the metaphor of menacing waters: we too cry "out of the depths" (Psalm 130:1). And we are right to do so – or so it seems to me, having once been startled by the waters of the pond in St Stephen's Green, in Dublin, Ireland, Europe, Earth, The Universe.

(March 2012)

Water World – Part II

A windstorm swept down on the lake, and the boat was filling
with water, and they were in danger. They went to him and
woke him up, shouting, "Master, Master, we are perishing!"
And he woke up and rebuked the wind and the raging waves;
they ceased, and there was a calm.
(Luke 8:22-25)

It was a children's Mass at Ballygall Parish, Dublin, and they were about to dramatize the storm at sea. A stretch of carpet before the altar was the boat, and two little ones were flapping a length of cloth between them for the raging waves of the sea. 'Jesus' gave a prodigious yawn and said, "Ah-aaah! I'm feeling very tired; I think I'll lie down in the boat for a while." "Good idea, Jesus!" an eight-year-old apostle replied; they stepped into the boat, and the adventure began.

Stories of Jesus and storms on the Sea of Galilee are found in all the Gospels (Luke 8:25; Matthew 8:23-27; 14:22-33; Mark 4:35-41; John 6:16-21). They usually end with the question, *"Who then is this, that he commands even the winds and the water, and they obey him?"* Isn't that God's job?

> *O Lord God of hosts,*
> *who is as mighty as you, O Lord?*
> *Your faithfulness surrounds you.*
> *You rule the raging of the sea;*
> *when its waves rise, you still them.*
> (Psalm 89:8-9; 104:5-13; 107:23-32)

Jesus and his fishermen friends shared the same Jewish understanding of the world; as they saw it, they lived in a space God had made in the Waters of the Deeps (Genesis 1:1-10). The sea their boat sailed on was the lapping of those Deep Waters at the boundaries of their lives. So when Jesus tamed wind and water, this was a power they respected: it was good to have him aboard, even if they were unsure who or what he was.

The evangelists, writing down these stories many decades later, believed they did know who Jesus was – their Lord and Saviour, whose resurrection they proclaimed. *"Do not be alarmed; you are looking for Jesus of Nazareth, who was crucified. He has been raised; he is not here"* (Mark 16:1-8; Luke 24; Matthew 28; John 20-21). In the light of that faith, the wonder was not that Jesus had power over the waters, but that the waters had power over

Detail of wax plaque showing the development of the human embryo. Early 19th century, probably made in Vienna, Austria.
(Image: ©Wellcome Trust/Science& Society)

him! Why was the Son of God risking his life in a small boat at sea in a storm?

The boat in a storm becomes an image of the Incarnation. In St Paul's telling of it, Christ Jesus was *in the form of God....but emptied himself, taking the form of a slave, being born in human likeness* (Philippians 2:6-11). Or, as St John wrote, the *Word became flesh and lived among us* (John 1:14). God not outside or above, but within the bubble of our existence. That had consequences: Jesus helpless in his mother's womb, waiting to be born; helpless on Calvary's cross, waiting to die.

This is a most amazing thing that we Christians believe, that the Divine should become part of creation in all its fragility and mortality. It is hard to credit and impossible to understand, and yet I go with the eight-year-old: "Good idea, Jesus!" If I truly believe that, then I too can step into the boat, and let the adventure begin.

(April 2012)

Water World – Part III

Then I saw a new heaven and a new earth;
for the first heaven and the first earth had passed away,
and the sea was no more.
(Revelation 21:1)

A child's voice I heard recently at the funeral Mass for a young man: "I hope Uncle Derek likes his new home in Heaven. Lord, hear us." Think of the layers of love and gracious wisdom that gave rise to that prayer, both in the child and the one who taught him!

Death was creation's gift to Christ. Once the Son of God became a human being and part of our created world, it was inevitable that he would die – that is what Incarnation means. But no one expected that he would rise from the dead. So the gospel began in the cry of Mary Magdalene racing back from the empty tomb: "I have seen the Lord" (John 20:1-18).

By the time of St Paul, about twenty-five years later writing to the Christians of Corinth, it was tradition: *"For I handed on to you as of first importance what I in turn had received: that Christ died for our sins in accordance with the scriptures, and that he was buried, and that he was raised on the third day in accordance with the scriptures"* (I Corinthians 15:3-4).

Not only "in accordance with the scriptures," but within the old Hebrew image of the world we live in: a space opened by God in the threatening Waters of the Deep, with Heaven above and the Underworld beneath (Genesis 1:1-10). This affects how we describe the events of our salvation; we say Jesus ascended into Heaven: *"as they were watching, he was lifted up, and a cloud took him out of their sight"* (Acts of the Apostles 1:9; Luke 24:51).

The death and resurrection of Jesus touched the entire creation, as the old thinking imagined it – Heaven above, and the bubble world in which we live, and the Underworld. St Paul quotes an early Christian hymn in which Jesus is exalted by God, *"so that at the name of Jesus / every knee should bend, / in heaven and on earth and under the earth"* (Philippians 2:6-11). Jesus is Lord of all people, all things, all creation.

According to the New Testament, this vast and generous faith has been held by the Church from the beginning; it reaches its climax in one of the final visions of the Bible: *"Then I saw a new heaven and a new earth; for the first heaven and the first earth had passed away, and the sea was no*

Crab Nebula: remains of a supernova witnessed in 1054 AD. It is 6,500 light years away.
(Image: ©NASA and ESA)

more" (Revelation 21:1-5). No more sea! No more Deep Waters, no more Flood. This too is "in accordance with the scriptures" and is the fulfilment of an ancient promise: *"the waters shall never again become a flood to destroy all flesh"* (Genesis 9:8-17).

The Bible tells us the story of our faith, and its language is shaped by the way it sees our world. We understand things differently now, and I wonder what language we might learn from the new visions of creation: of relativity, quantum physics, evolution, and a 13.7 billion year old universe, more vast than we can imagine and in which humanity has occupied only a tiny corner and a few moments of time.

Whatever we learn, I hope it can be told with the same simplicity and wonder as the prayer of a child for a lost uncle.

(May 2012)

7: Stories

As It Happened

This whole collection is slightly autobiographical, but this section is more overtly so. Each article arose out of a personal experience: I have been enriched by many people over my life, for which I give deep thanks.

The Door of My Lips

Rescue me, Lord, from the wicked;
from the violent keep me safe,
from those who plan evil in their hearts
and stir up strife every day;
who sharpen their tongue like an adder's
with the poison of viper on their lips.
(Psalm 140)

I gave a lift to a man once in County Clare in Ireland, who asked me if I were a musician. I said, "No, I'm not," but why did he ask? "You have a musicianer's hands," he said. I suppose he meant that they were soft! "Are you a musician?" I asked. "Yes," he played the tin whistle. "Will you play now?" "I will indeed, sir," and he took out a tin whistle from his jacket and began to play. The music was lovely, but I noticed that whenever we came upon anyone walking the road, my companion would stop, put down the tin whistle, and would resume playing only after we had passed. Was it shyness or fear? He was a cattle drover, and by his own account had often been badly treated; and though I didn't learn much else of his story, I wondered at what might have been done or said to him to make him so.

It is so easy to take away someone's happiness; a word would do it, or a jibe. Do you remember the childhood rhyme: Sticks and stones may break your bones, but names will never hurt you? Don't believe a word of it! Ask the child who is being crushed by a nickname. Or being taunted about colour or national origin or, God forbid!, a physical or mental deformity. Or someone whose life has been destroyed by a lie. You don't have much left after they have taken away your good name. It happens on a massive scale in wartime propaganda, but it is also found in schools and work places, and even closer to home and to church. Small wonder so many of the psalms fear the liar, the mocker, the betrayer, the perjurer:

They sharpen their tongues like swords;
they aim bitter words like arrows.
(Psalm 64 and Psalms 12, 35, 109)

In the mouth of a bully, words can be as bad as a beating, and they don't leave a mark, at least not on the body.

So, there we were: two strangers travelling together, sharing by chance a short stretch of life's journey. I found myself admiring my companion's courage, the spirit in him that defied the ghosts by music-making. Whatever else, they hadn't been able to take that from him. After I had dropped him off, I was thinking how similar we all are, how equally vulnerable: that any of us can suffer the hurt of a tongue-lashing or a snide remark or a falsehood or a betrayal. But mostly I wondered at the harm that I myself could do or, again, any of us, through what we say. Words are dangerous. The Hebrews, the original singers of the psalms, believed that words once uttered took on a life of their own, a power that put them beyond our control. You couldn't take them back. Do I even know what harm I may have done by things I said that were callous or harsh or false? I might need help with such a wayward gift as speech. The Psalms had a prayer for that too:

Set, O Lord, a guard over my mouth;
keep watch, O Lord, at the door of my lips. (Psalm 141)

Making sweet music as represented by this man in a batik from Togo in West Africa. With every breath God gives me, what music do I make with my lips – do my words build up and comfort?

(September/October 2002)

I pay tribute to The Stella, a small cinema in Dublin that showed the movie of "The Lord of the Rings" in matinee performances months after it had gone from other, grander establishments, thus giving missionaries on home leave in the Summer months a chance to see it on a big screen. I told you this was personal!

The Young Lion and The Dragon

**For you God has commanded the angels
to keep you in all your ways.
They shall bear you upon their hands
lest you strike your foot against a stone.
On the lion and the viper you will tread
and trample the young lion and the dragon.**
(Psalm 91)

All those many years ago, when I gave my life away in signing up to be a missionary priest with St Patrick's, I had very little idea what demands of courage or generosity or stamina or faith it might entail. And I most certainly never imagined that it would one day mean that I would be on mission in Africa, nowhere near a cinema, while *The Lord of the Rings* was playing to packed audiences on the big screens back home in Ireland. All right, all right: I've a lot to worry me! But I had loved the book, and when I finally did get to see it I loved the film as well.

It is a story told on a grand scale, epic, mythical: the struggle between Good and Evil, between the forces of light and of darkness. It celebrates all that is most noble in us – brave and chivalrous men, valiant and beautiful women, and the great-hearted Hobbits and Elves and Dwarves and other peoples that shared the imaginary Earth of the story. The enemies are monstrous, led by a foul Lord of Evil who threatens all that is good in the world: the future hangs in the balance – and in the story, it is we ourselves, and our times, that are that future.

Sometimes the Word of God in the Bible sounds in a similar epic mode: there are dragons and monsters in the Book of Revelation. Psalm 91 also speaks of dragons, and of lions and vipers and terrors and plagues and scourges – and of angels who come to help us. The world is a dangerous place; we can be overwhelmed by the gaze of our enemies:

*Their eyes are watching to strike me to the ground,
as though they were lions ready to claw
or like some young lion crouched in hiding.*
(Psalm 17)

For one New Testament writer, *"our struggle is not against enemies of blood and flesh, but against the rulers, against the authorities, against the cosmic powers of this present darkness, against the spiritual forces of evil in the heavenly places"* (Ephesians 6:12).

It is not that *The Lord of the Rings* is larger than life: more that our own lives are larger than, perhaps, we realise. Our hearts are stirred and ennobled by the story's great deeds and, yet, we fight the same battles ourselves. The choices people make every day – to be loving, to be true, to stand up to mockery and bullying and corruption, not to lose heart – are often secret and unsung. But it is just this domestic valour that does most to bring hope to the world. The real heroes and heroines are ordinary people, though they are not often honoured; I find it is their lives that most inspire me. This, too, is at the core of the story. As it is of the gospel: *"for all of them have contributed out of their abundance, but she out of her poverty has put in all she had to live on"* (Luke 21).

This cloth painting from Nigeria depicts four lions.

(March 2003)

Yesterday's Man

Now that I am old and grey-headed,
do not forsake me, God.
Let me tell of your power to all ages,
praise your strength and justice to the skies,
tell of you who have worked such wonders.
O God, who is like you?
(Psalm 71:18-19)

Just now I am in the process of leaving a position I have held for the past twelve years, handing over the responsibility and access of a leadership role in our Society – a big job, too! At times I feel free and relieved, at times empty-handed. To be honest, I'm glad to be rid of it, and yet I'll miss it – there is a sense of having let go something that gave me some satisfaction and pride in myself. Now I'm moving on, stepping down, getting out of the way. Lame duck. Yesterday's man.

I wouldn't want to make too big a meal of this: it's small cheese compared to what happens to many people when they lose something that had filled their lives – when your children grow up and away from you, when they have slaughtered your entire dairy herd because of foot-and-mouth disease, when you return from the wars and the famines to find that nobody wants to know, when your skills – and you along with them – have become obsolete. Or, you are sidelined by sickness or retirement or old age:
"Do not reject me now that I am old;
when my strength fails do not forsake me."
(Psalm 71)
You can feel you're in the way, and out of it, at the same time.

There was a time when Jesus was out of it. Do you recall the forlorn complaint of the two on the way to Emmaus a couple of days after he died on the cross? *"But we had hoped that he was the one to set Israel free"* (Luke 24). We had hoped! More disappointment, another futile hero, yesterday's man.

Sometimes a song will modulate from one key or tempo to another: a new beat, a new song, bringing a new energy. Perhaps that is what I'm feeling in my life. It's about change, which may be for better or worse but will come anyway. It can happen in a heartbeat or, as with the drifting of continents, at the pace at which our fingernails grow.

The young dance under an ebony tree, and the old have an honoured place in this batik from the Ivory Coast in West Africa.

At any rate, there is no change without loss and letting go. So I am taking a break before my next appointment: I have a lot to learn, and need to know more about what is changing in the world, and what has changed – or not changed – in myself. I may belong to yesterday more than I think. What have I still to let go of?

These are times of war and rumours of war – some things don't change! But it is also Easter time, and the word on the street is that he has risen! There is a new heartbeat, and a new song, and a hope for us all. *"Jesus Christ is the same yesterday and today and forever"* (Hebrew 13). Good news, for a change.

(May 2003)

I wrote this shortly after staying in Jerusalem on sabbatical; I think it was a kind of blessing – in fact, the whole sabbatical was!

A Narrow Place

"Answer me when I call, O God of my right!
You gave me room when I was in distress.
Be gracious to me, and hear my prayer."
(Psalm 4:2 NRSV)

Jerusalem was clogged with people up for the holiday. I was pushing my way through the narrow streets, always it seemed against the flow. I was anxious and fretful and feeling crowded in, and it must have shown on my face. Suddenly, a child stepped directly in front of me, looked up at me, and put a most ferocious scowl on her face. I burst out laughing – what else could I do? She grinned, and stepped around me and ran off after her pals. I felt my face and my spirit relaxing: all at once there seemed to be more room on the streets, and I could move freely. A simple, mysterious, amazing moment.

The Hebrew Psalms have a range of terms that we translate as troubles and distress and anguish. The image behind these words – the root meaning, if you like – has to do with being hemmed in, crushed, compressed. Situations in which you have no options, no power to resist or to escape: a terminal sickness, or a fear, or a collapsed relationship, or a life gone out of control. At the heart of anguish is the conviction that there is no hope, that you are trapped in *"a narrow place, where there is no way to turn either to the right hand or to the left"* (Numbers 22:26).

What would salvation be in such a case? There are other words in the psalms that come out in English as help or save or deliver or enlarge; they have a root meaning of making space, giving room, opening a way.
"You gave me a wide place for my steps under me,
and my feet did not slip." (Psalm 18:36 NRSV)
Or, as was said of God's dealings with Job,
"He also allured you out of distress into a broad place where there was no constraint" (Job 36:16).

I suppose the foundation image behind all this, for the Hebrews at least, is their Exodus story – how God opened a space in the Red Sea for them to pass from slavery to freedom (Exodus 14:21-29). It is one of the great metaphors for what God does.

The foundation image of our faith is another Exodus story, the death and resurrection of Jesus. He lived under the same constraints as we do. In the old, extreme phrase, *"he was obedient unto death, even death on a cross"* (Philippians 2:8). He entered the narrow place. Sooner or later we all do. Whether at times during our existence or at its end, we share the same diminishment as Jesus, the same narrowing of life.

At his death Jesus prayed to his Father: *"Into your hands I commend my spirit"* (Psalm 31:5; Luke 23:46). And the psalm continues:
"You who have seen my affliction and taken heed of my soul's distress, have not handed me over to the enemy, but set my feet at large" (Psalm 31:8-9).

Batik from Israel: The City of Jerusalem with its crowded buildings and narrow streets.

(June 2004)

Desert in the Heart

I remember the days that are past:
I ponder all your works.
I muse on what your hand has wrought
and to you I stretch out my hands.
Like a parched land my soul thirsts for you.
(Psalm 143)

I have a jotter that I hope does not fall into the wrong hands; it contains two lists I made during a sabbatical recently. As I looked back over my life as a priest and a missionary, I wanted to write down what I felt had been good or bad, life giving or damaging. What had I achieved, in myself and in my work; what had I drawn back from, or hadn't had the wit or the grace or the guts to do? How had I been with my friends – and my enemies? I filled eighteen pages, about evenly divided between positive and negative. You see what I mean about falling into the wrong hands!

I was looking for patterns. I have been a priest for many years now, and I know I can 'Talk the Talk'; but I suspected that the patterns I would see in my life and behaviour might be a better indicator of who and what I had become. More like the 'real me'. The things I had listed told me about my priorities, and helped me to recognise what stretched me the most, what produced the worst heartbreaks, and what gave me the most satisfaction in my chosen vocation. What were the sufferings I kept inflicting on myself, and the empty, desert areas I occasionally sensed in my heart.

Then, I gathered my jotter and its eighteen pages of my life, and brought them to the Sacrament of Penance. I thought there might be more to what I was doing than mere self-knowledge or self-improvement:
"You desire truth in the inward being;
therefore teach me wisdom in my secret heart."
(Psalm 51:6 NRSV)

I suppose I realised that sooner or later I would need to converse with God on all of this, and the Sacrament was as good a meeting ground as any. It is a place where you can safely be yourself.

So I went through the lists – or a summary of them – with a wise, patient confessor. He helped me to see the areas where healing was called for, or which might need some forgiveness and more acceptance. But we ended up talking about thirst; he was an Ethiopian, and knew about deserts and drought:

In this batik
from Kenya,
East Africa,
two women
gather water,
a vital daily
task in desert
areas.

"O God, you are my God, for you I long;
for you my soul is thirsting.
My body pines for you
like a dry, weary land without water."
(Psalm 63:1)

If there are desert areas within me, it is partly due to neglect – that happens! But it is also because we all have a desert in our hearts, a longing and a thirst that draws us beyond ourselves. And I, for one, am not sufficiently or often enough aware of that. The Sacrament can be a good place to find such awareness. Or so I believe.

(July/August 2004)

In 2003 and 2004 I spent four months on sabbatical in the Holy Land – a huge privilege, and also a time of insight and revelations for all of us on the course.

Jerusalem

I rejoiced when I heard them say:
"Let us go to God's house."
And now our feet are standing
within your gates, O Jerusalem.
(Psalm 122)

The immigration official – they are notoriously strict and unbending in Israel – looked up from my papers, smiled and said, "Happy birthday!" So it was: I was sixty-six years old the day I first entered Jerusalem. I couldn't get enough of it – this place with, as someone once said, its history and geography of salvation: *Jerusalem! The mountains surround her, so the Lord surrounds his people both now and for ever* (Psalm 125).

There were eighteen of us on a four-month course in the Holy Land. We lived in the Muslim Quarter of the Old City of Jerusalem, amid centuries of history. *Of you are told glorious things, O city of God!* (Psalm 87). And terrible things: this is possibly the most fought-over strip of land in the world. There are dark scars here in the fabric and people of the city.

But it may be that the deepest wounds lie outside the Land of Israel. There is a long and savage history of Christian anti-Semitism, but nothing matches the magnitude of what was done to the Jews in Europe in the twentieth century. I was a child when some of these things were happening. I grew up not knowing a single Jew! There weren't many in Ireland, and though Jews do have an honoured place in our country's story, Ireland was ungenerous in accepting them even as refugees from Nazi Germany.

In Jerusalem we saw the grave of Oskar Schindler in a Catholic cemetery, and the trees planted in memory of the Righteous Gentiles who had supported Jews and the State of Israel. We also visited **Yad Vashem**, the Holocaust Memorial Museum – but I have no words to describe that. *They have poured out blood like water in Jerusalem; no one is left to bury the dead. We have become the taunt of our neighbours* (Psalm 79).

Living in Jerusalem and experiencing Jewish life made me more aware of the Jewish roots of Christianity. I thought of what Jesus said to the Samaritan woman, that "salvation comes from the Jews" (John 4:22). As did Jesus himself, and his family and first followers. *Zion shall be called*

'Mother' / for all shall be her children (Psalm 87). And yet, the Holocaust and the deaths of six million Jews.

And here I noticed an interesting thing. There were eleven different nationalities in our small group: seven Asians from South Korea, Japan, India, and the Philippines; one African from Tanzania; and the rest you might loosely call "Europeans", from Ireland, Scotland, Slovakia, Poland, Canada, and Australia. And it was among these last that I found the greatest concern about anti-Semitism. The evil history of hatred against the Jews is a European perversion, the guilt of Christendom stretching from Portugal across to Russia and beyond. For the Asians and the Africans it was different: this was not part of their story nor of their Christian heritage. They may have their own horrors to contemplate and regret, but not this one. It is important for us who come from Europe to preach the Gospel to remember this. *If I forget you, Jerusalem, let my right hand wither...if I prize not Jerusalem above all my joys!* (Psalm 137).

"Pray for the peace of Jerusalem" (Psalm 122). The batik comes from Israel.

(June 2005)

The Child In My Arms

Whoever welcomes one such child in my name
welcomes me.
(Matthew 18:5)

I became aware of the child by my side, about a year and a half old, looking tensely up at me and with her arms stretched out to be lifted. Which I did; she immediately flung her arms around my neck and clung to me. No cry, no word, no sound. It was after Mass last Sunday, and I had been gathering things at the altar. I looked down the church: people were still moving about, meetings getting started, the choir packing up music sheets and instruments; and a woman sitting about halfway down smiling at me – I guessed she must be the mother. I wandered down her way and looked my question: the child had just had an injection. Ah! I had forgotten – a medical team was at the back of the church giving Meningitis vaccinations. It's a painful one: I know – I had one myself a few months ago. The child wasn't ready yet to go back to her mother, so I carried her around a bit more, chatting with some other people, she still clinging to me, her head on my shoulder. By the time I got back again to where the mother was, her sister – about eight or nine years old – had arrived, and the child willingly went to her: that would be very normal here. Still no cry, no word, no sound. I have no idea why she had chosen to come to me.

Now, this could go in any of several different directions. I could ask a provocative question: whether I, a priest, could do such a thing in Ireland? Would I dare? With all the horror and betrayal and damage done, what have we lost, priests, people, Church, children? Is it too soon to ask what has been gained? Some redress and healing for harmed people, and a stop to the abuses? Maybe a more wholesome idea of what a church should be? Because what we have to say is still worth saying.

Or I could wonder about Africa, where I am called "Reverend Father". African society values family very highly, and the ideal of "Father" resonates with strength, responsibility, affection and a wish to share. But Africa also has experience of the "Big Man" with power and unquestioned dominance and a desire to control. Which will have the greater influence on us, who are priests and bishops of the Church in Africa? What kind of "Fathers" will we be?

Or I could raise the whole incident to a higher level, as the prophet Hosea tended to do, and reflect on God as Mother and Father, comforting us in our pain:

I took them up in my arms; but they did not know that I healed them....I was to them like those who lift infants to their cheeks. I bent down to them and fed them (Hosea 11:3,4). Jesus taught us to call God "Father" – what was he telling us?

Or I could examine my own reactions to what happened, my own feelings: glad that I was able to hold and comfort her, and was trusted to do so; tenderness at her pain, and an old ache that this wasn't my child, that there would never be for me a "my child". And a grief that even this can be distorted and destroyed. I was also laughing at myself: what would a 68-year old virgin know about any of it? Still, I do know a blessing when I'm given one. To tell you the truth, I was sorry to let her go.

Ink drawing of Yoruba man with child by Nigerian artist, Kehinde Babatunde.

(July/August 2006)

What I describe here was neither war nor famine, but it was the action of a government against its own people. Legal or illegal, it was a harsh, dry, hopeless time.

Harmattan

Deliver us, O Lord, from our bondage
as streams in dry land.
Those who are sowing in tears
will sing when they reap.
(Psalm 126)

It is more than two months since we've had any rain. That's normal: this is the dry season, and it will be several months yet before the rains return. The land is dry, and dead grass stands in long withered stalks waiting to be gathered for thatching. Dust covers everything, especially from the harmattan – vast clouds of microscopic particles that drift down from the Sahara, a dry fog that leaches the colours from the landscape: *"a dry weary land without water"* (Psalm 63). It can close airports, and is so dry that it warps timber and cracks the spines of books. (I'm told it made a rare appearance in Cork in Ireland some years ago, where they called it "Fallout"!)

But the harmattan is in our hearts these days, and in our parish. On the edges of new cities in many places in the world, development can be haphazard and unplanned and so it was here in this fringe area. Over several decades people have been allowed to build with the tacit agreement of local authorities and traditional rulers, but with little provision of services or roads. Shanty towns: what sociologists would describe as "informal settlements". Others prefer the term "illegal squatters" – that makes it criminal, and easier to justify moving them on. But these are civil servants, carpenters, doctors, home-makers, teachers, traders, and the many unemployed attracted to the city. Then the bulldozers came: Judgement Day!

By Christmas two thirds of our people were gone, their homes and businesses demolished. Places of worship, Christian and Muslim, had gone down too – the remnant celebrated under an open sky: in the dry season, that was possible, appropriate, even enjoyable. But we felt uneasy, somehow estranged from the place:
O how could we sing
the song of the Lord
on alien soil? (Psalm 137)

What is it that can make the land become alien beneath your very feet?

This is a new city, and in many ways a beautiful and well-planned one. It is a capital city, yet some seem to regard it as the preserve of the powerful and the privileged. But the soul of a city – or a country – is to be found not just in the favoured few but in all its people: the great and the lowly, the needy and the gifted, the good and the bad. They should be welcomed, helped and housed – not brutally excluded. *"If the Lord does not watch over the city, in vain do the watchers keep vigil"* (Psalm 127).

In Nature, as we know, the seasons turn, the rains will come again. But would it be so in "the affairs of men"? I do not know where they have all gone to, nor what will become of those still remaining. Some were overwhelmed; yet these are a resilient people, with courage and fortitude. And they have not entirely lost hope:
But God changes desert into streams,
thirsty ground into springs of water.
There the hungry are settled,
and they build a city to dwell in.
(Psalm 107)

(May 2007)

"Two women in a town during harmattan; only the fruit they carry show any colour." Oil painting by Taiwo Lawal from Nigeria.

165

Body Work

Something which has existed since the beginning,
that we have heard,
and we have seen with our own eyes;
that we have watched
and touched with our hands:
the Word, who is life.
(I John 1:1)

Some years ago I had a full body massage, the kind of thing that footballers and athletes and clients at health farms have as a matter of course. I found it an overwhelming experience. Small wonder: by the nature of things, and my calling as a priest, my "touch history" (as a friend put it) has been rather sparse.

Later that day, celebrating Mass, I came to the words, "This is my body" – and was stopped in my tracks. I thought of the body, and how it can be treated. How bodies are marked and misshaped by accident or design or age or sickness or abuse. There are women and children all over the world whose bodies have become commodities to be sold and savaged. Even custom and tradition may mark the body: the Gbagy women of Northern Nigeria do not usually carry loads on their heads, but on their upper backs; it can distort the spine as the body adjusts itself to bear the weight.

I thought of the body-beautiful, and the face and form that can enchant you across a lifetime. The noble way Africa's women carry themselves, *"our daughters graceful as columns adorned as though for a palace"* (Psalm 144:12). The wonder and mystery of the human body and the things it does.

And I thought of the body of those we love: the body we recognise and hold and cherish and care for, *"that we have watched and touched with our hands."* And the dying body that carries my dear one away.

Ink drawings from Nigeria.

And I thought, this is my body, the Word made flesh, *"the Word, who is life."* Bodies wear out, and come to an end: what happens then is another matter. But whatever glorious thing it is, it happens to the body too. Perhaps that is why we care for the bodies of the dead: *"They took the body of Jesus and wrapped it with the spices in linen cloths, according to the burial custom of the Jews"* (John 19:40).

I pulled myself together, and got on with the Mass; for there too we watch, and touch with our hands, the Word, who is life. Maybe my "touch history" is not quite as sparse as I had supposed.

(April 2008)

This was completed during a difficult time in our parish, as is clear from the article itself. Writing it was a kind of relief, a therapy, a prayer. But what most remains in my heart is the kindness of people.

Old Reliable

O praise the Lord, all you nations,
acclaim God all you peoples!
Strong is God's love for us;
the Lord is faithful for ever.
(Psalm 117)

The car I drive is about ten years old; the model is at least twenty-five years old: a Peugeot 504 saloon – they were still being assembled and sold here long after they had disappeared from the motor showrooms of Europe. A strong car with large wheels and high clearance, great for rough roads. One day I drove into a neighbouring parish, and a woman by the church steps called over to me: "Old Reliable!" She meant the car.

There are two words, a matching pair, that travel in tandem through the Hebrew scriptures: *love and faithfulness*, **chesed** and **'emet**. These are dense words, packed with meaning, and are often translated in different ways: love can also come out in our English versions as "mercy" or "kindness"; *faithfulness* could be "constancy" or "truth". *Your merciful love and your truth will always guard me* (Psalm 40:10-11; 57:10; 89:14; 100:5; 115:1). The translations may vary, but the basic assurance remains: God won't let you down. Old Reliable.

But neither will God always do just as we ask; the psalms are full of that too. *Why do you hide your face? Why do you forget our affliction and oppression?* (Psalm 44:24; 88:14). God figures in the blame game – there are what insurers call "Acts of God".
> *For God spoke and summoned the gale,*
> *tossing the waves of the sea*
> *up to heaven and back into the deep.*
> (Psalm 107:25-26)
God does not spare us the declines and disasters of life; we grow old and weak and sick – we die, our prayers unanswered. Injustice flourishes. What price "Old Reliable" then?

I began writing this several months ago, but it lapsed for a while, and now I am finishing it in Holy Week when God's reliability is tested to the extreme. A friend and colleague, Fr. Joe Purcell, a St. Patrick missionary,

Batik from Mauritius.

died suddenly here two days ago, and what fills my heart is the kindness of people. The "correct compassion" (as a poet named it) of doctors and nurses. The load-bearing dependability of friends. The tears of people. **chesed** and **'emet**, *love* and *faithfulness*.

It seems to me that God's love and faithfulness course all through our lives; they bring out the best in us, and at the worst of times. It may even be that God's work is best done through the love and faithfulness of ordinary people, so simply given that we might not recognize the gift for what it really is – the hope of the world.

In the end of his own story, **chesed** and **'emet** were all Jesus had to rely on:

> *Into your hand I commit my spirit;*
> *you have redeemed me, O Lord, faithful God.*
> (Psalm 31:5; Luke 23:46)

Faithful God! Old Reliable!

(July/August 2009)

Writing this was a sheer pleasure, it is such a gracious story – the incident itself of the compassion of Christ, and the adventure of the narrative: it could so easily have been suppressed or lost, as I'm sure much else has been.

Grace Notes

**The scribes and the Pharisees brought a woman
who had been caught in adultery...**
(John 7:53 – 8:11)

A s a child I was put to learning the piano. I was an indifferent student, and my frustrated teacher would write notes on the sheet music for my parents to read: *"A very lazy boy, can't play a scale or piece"*, and *"Not known yet after 6 months."* More than sixty-five years later these incriminating documents are still extant and in my sister's possession; from time to time some of her grandchildren – who are very diligent students of both trumpet and piano – ask to see the messages on the margins of the music.

There is also a single-sheet letter from my father in Mountjoy jail internment camp, dated August 27th, 1923, shortly after the end of the Irish civil war – a letter to his mother at home in Waterford. It was, of course, censored, but there is a note on the back from a humane Prison Adjutant, Captain N. A. Ryan: "A Chara, I would advise you to get the OC, Waterford to communicate with the Military Governor Mountjoy Prison – regarding your son's arrest."

Over a thousand years ago, Irish monks had the habit of writing notes on the manuscripts they were copying: *"A blessing on the soul of Fergus! I am very cold"*, or the happier *"Sunday of a warm Easter."* Or a gloss written one stormy night as Viking pirates were forced to stay in harbour, and the monasteries were safe from looting:
The wind is wild tonight.
It tosses the sea's white hair.
What harm ... It is calm seas
bring the sharp warriors from the North.

These are all marginal stories, grace notes to the music of life, dependant on more substantial records for their survival. Such stories can be lost; it almost happened to the story of a woman who was brought to Jesus for judgement, as told in the Gospel according to John.

She was hauled before him and accused of committing adultery; a capital offence, her accusers claimed. Jesus ignored them, except to suggest that they might kill her themselves, if they thought they were good enough. They showed what they thought by slinking away. The woman remained, with no sign of repentance, no extenuating circumstances, no word from Jesus that it was her faith that saved her, not even a partner in crime who could share the blame. Guilty as charged, thrown on the mercy of the court. And that is what she got from Jesus, with the remark that she might consider mending her ways.

A wonderful story, but in fact it is not found in the earliest and most reliable manuscripts of John's Gospel; nor was it written by the same hand that wrote that Gospel. Whoever recorded the incident, it seems it survived for centuries, more or less unattached, before it was accepted into John, Chapter 8 where it is usually placed today. From the margins it moved into the heart of the narrative. It had secured tenure, you might say, but what took it so long?

There is a suggestion that there were some in the early days of the Church who felt that a sterner attitude towards adultery was called for; that Jesus was too tolerant, too free with his forgiveness. The story was an embarrassment, so that they were reluctant to include it in the gospel narrative. Too amazing a grace? And yet, this story of a greater mercy survived. I think it is as well for us that it did – the generosity of God was always a challenge to us.

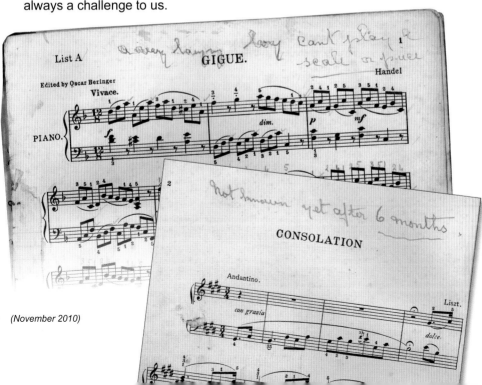

(November 2010)

I have to admit I had fun writing this. I suggest you read 1 Samuel 17 about David and Goliath: despite the blood and gore, there is fun there too. See the exchange between David and his older brother Eliab, verses 28-30.

end bag

He ordered them to take nothing for their journey except a staff; no bread, no bag, no money in their belts; but to wear sandals and not to put on two tunics.
(Mark 6:8-9)

A year ago, passing through Gatwick airport in England, when I collected my checked-in luggage it had a label attached to it which proclaimed in fluorescent orange, **end bag**. This was new to me: were the baggage handlers – experts in these matters – telling me the bag was past its best, and should now be decently retired, or put down? **END BAG!** On enquiry, however, I learned it was simply a tag put on the last item of luggage off-loaded from the hold of the aircraft. No need to expect any more – this is the end bag.

In more recent times I have taken to travelling with hand-luggage only. This is not out of any excess of virtue, or detachment from the things of this world; simply that I am tired of wrestling with several suitcases, or standing in long queues to be weighed and measured. I try to carry only what I have to, and trust there will be a clean shirt at the end of the journey. In this I claim an odd kinship with David, son of Jesse, in the First Book of Samuel, Chapter 17.

The young David is about to face the Philistine warrior-giant Goliath in single combat and, as if to relieve the tension in the narrative, there is a moment of farce. To kit him out for the contest, King Saul *"clothed David with his armour; he put a bronze helmet on his head and clothed him with a coat of mail. David strapped Saul's sword over the armour, and he tried in vain to walk..."* (I Samuel 17:38-40). He couldn't move for the weight he was carrying. In the end, he took only his sling and a pouch for stones – the ultimate in hand-luggage? (Though in today's airport anxiety even that would probably be regarded as too dangerous to be allowed on board.) The clean shirt? After Goliath had been defeated and killed, Saul's son Jonathan *"stripped himself of the robe that he was wearing, and gave it to David"* (I Samuel 18:4).

Jesus told his disciples to take no bag at all on their journey: *"... no bread, no bag, no money in their belts"* (Mark 6:8). This is a severe and spare injunction, and I can't say that I have often witnessed it. And perhaps there is an alternative generosity in carrying things for others to enjoy; that is certainly a common thing among missionaries that I know.

There is another kind of baggage we can carry with us, more deeply embedded in our lives and our persons, and not so easily left behind – hurts, grudges, prejudices, and obsessions we have acquired. Some of these we know about, some we are not aware of, but they weigh us down all the same. Like the suited-up David, sometimes we clunk around and try in vain to walk. We may need to learn what we should let go, in order to get anywhere at all. Maybe that is what Jesus meant: not what we carry in our hands but in our hearts.

One way or another, on our final journey – which we have already begun – we will have to let go of everything. The end bag will be an empty one, and we will stand alone, cherished and called.

(September/October 2009)

Scripture Citation Index

A Select Index of Topics – to supplement Contents, pages v – vii.

Acknowledgements and Permissions

Pages 1, 12, 13: "Sing Out, My Soul" from *All Desires Known*, Third Edition Copyright © 1998, 1992, 2006 by Janet Morley. Used by permission of Morehouse Publishing, an imprint of Church Publishing Incorporated, and of SPCK. www.churchpublishing.org

Pages 11 and 83: Images ©Vie de JESUS MAFA, 24 Rue du Maréchal Joffre, 7800 Versailles, France www.jesusmafa.com

Page 19: Enamel courtesy of Anne Murphy (©Anne Murphy Ireland) www.eala-enamels.com

Page 22: *Caoineadh na dTrí Muire* (Lament of the Three Marys) translated by Fr. Des Forristal, by kind permission of *The Columba Press* www.columba.ie

Page 82: *"Concerning the Divine Word" from Poems of St. John of the Cross*, translated by Roy Campbell, Harvill Press

Page 124: Quotation from *Hogfather* by Terry Pratchett (©1996 HarperTorch) Kind permission of Ralph M. Vicinanza Ltd, PO Box 464, Dobbs Ferry, NY 10522, USA

Page 62 and 128: *Now The Green Blade Riseth* used by permission of Church Publishing Incorporated www.churchpublishing.org

Page 147: Detail of wax plaque ©Wellcome Trust/Science & Society Science & Society Picture Library, Science Museum Group, Exhibition Road, London SW7 2DD, England. Used with permission. www.scienceandsociety.co.uk

Page 149: Crab Nebula Image ©NASA and ESA

The author and publisher gratefully acknowledge the permission granted to reproduce the copyright material in this book. Every effort has been made to trace copyright holders and to obtain their permission for the use of copyright material. The publisher apologizes for any errors or omissions in the above list and would be grateful if notified of any corrections that should be incorporated in future reprints or editions of this book.